Incubating and Hatching Homegrown Chicks

Perpetuate a Self-Sufficient Backyard Flock!

Anna Hess

Contents

Introduction

A muffled peep comes from a pristine egg. The egg vibrates gently as the fully-formed chick inside pushes its way into the air sac at the blunt end, then knocks against the inner wall of the shell with its egg tooth to make a breathing hole into the outside world.

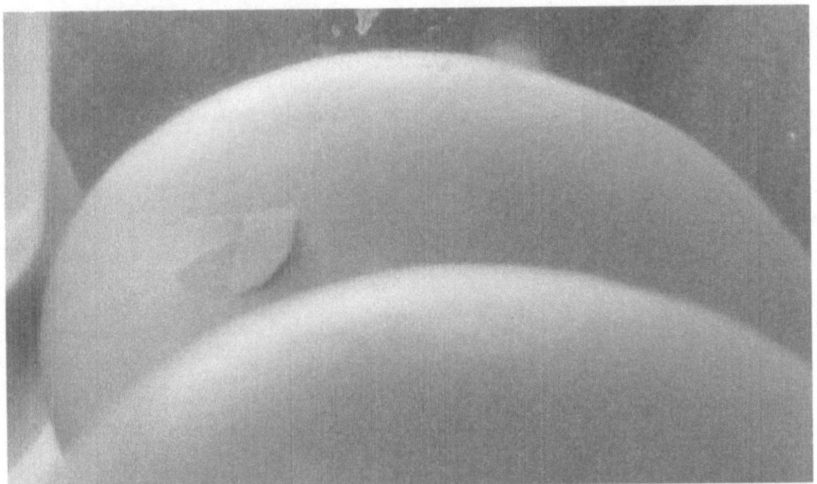

I watch with bated breath for seven hours. Nothing. I would have thought that the chick had perished if I couldn't see the membrane around its tiny beak flutter in the air currents of the chick's breathing. The baby chicken is only resting from its exertions and preparing for the most difficult adventure of its life to date.

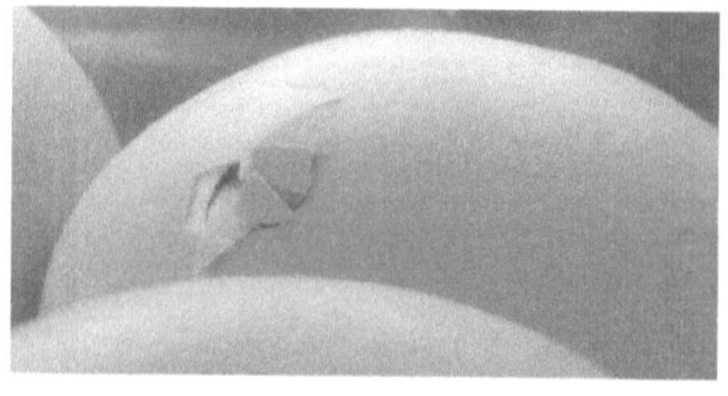

With sudden vigor, the chick goes back to work, whacking its face against the boundary of its minuscule world.

The unzipping process has begun. Piece by piece, the chick knocks a circle of shell fragments out of its way, cutting the top off the egg.

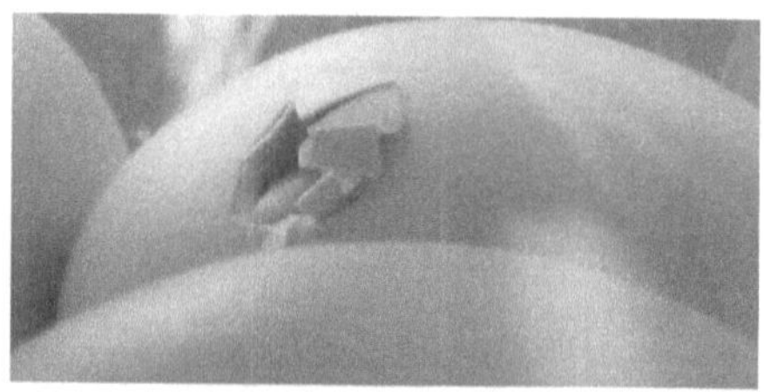

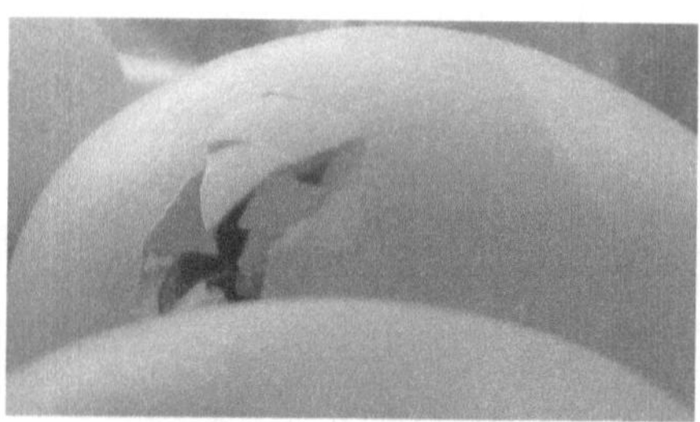

Once in the groove, the chick no longer stops to rest, except for brief breathers during which it peeps adamantly. "I'm coming out!", I imagine the youngster saying.

Within half an hour, the shell has nearly split in two.

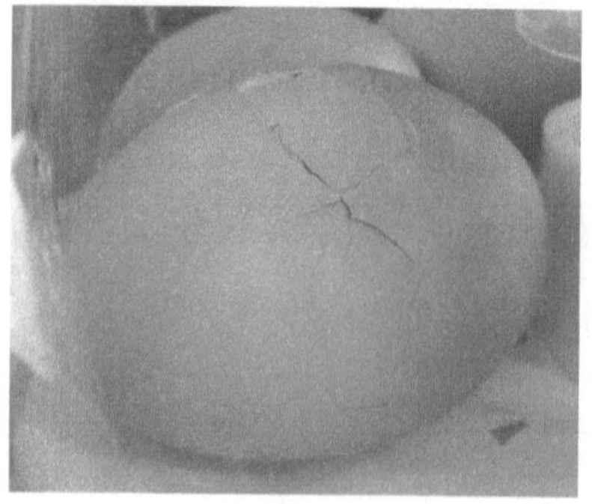

Rather than laboriously rotating its body so it can continue pecking at the shell, the chick now puts its strong legs to work. Bracing its head against the blunt end of the shell and its feet against the pointed end, it puuuuuushes...

I can see sodden feathers through the crack, and I gasp in awe.

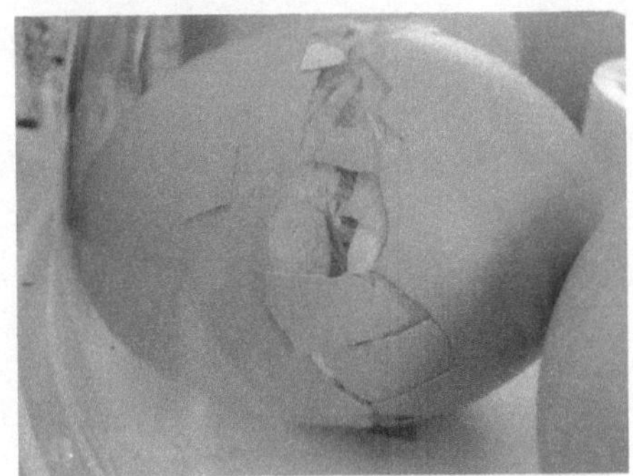

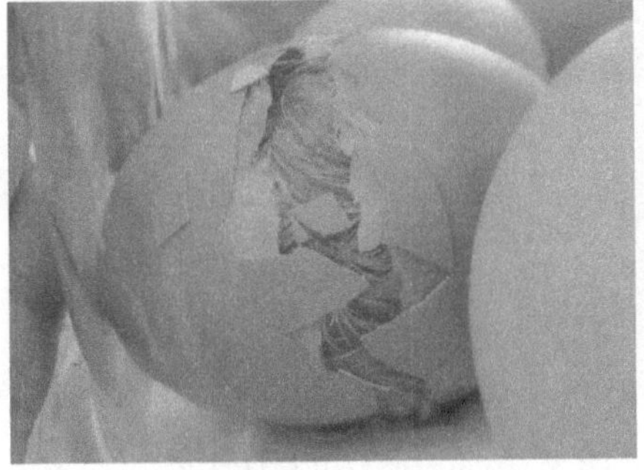

The egg begins to roll against its neighbors from the force of the chick's exertions.

Yet more chick becomes visible unti l... *plop*! The baby bird falls out onto the floor of the incubator.

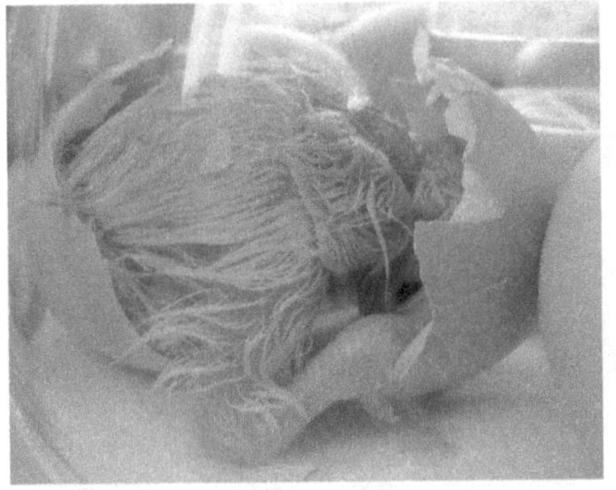

All that effort has worn the poor chick out, so it lies there partially emerged for several minutes while it peeps ecstatically.

Then, with a massive flapping of incipient wings, the chick is free to drape itself across its unhatched siblings.

I'll never forget the excitement and drama of my first hatch. But I also remember the emotionally difficult aftermath when our first vibrant chick accidentally speared one of its later-hatching siblings with a toenail, killing the youngster immediately. Other chicks didn't even make it to the unzipping stage and I knew that their fatalities were (mostly) my fault.

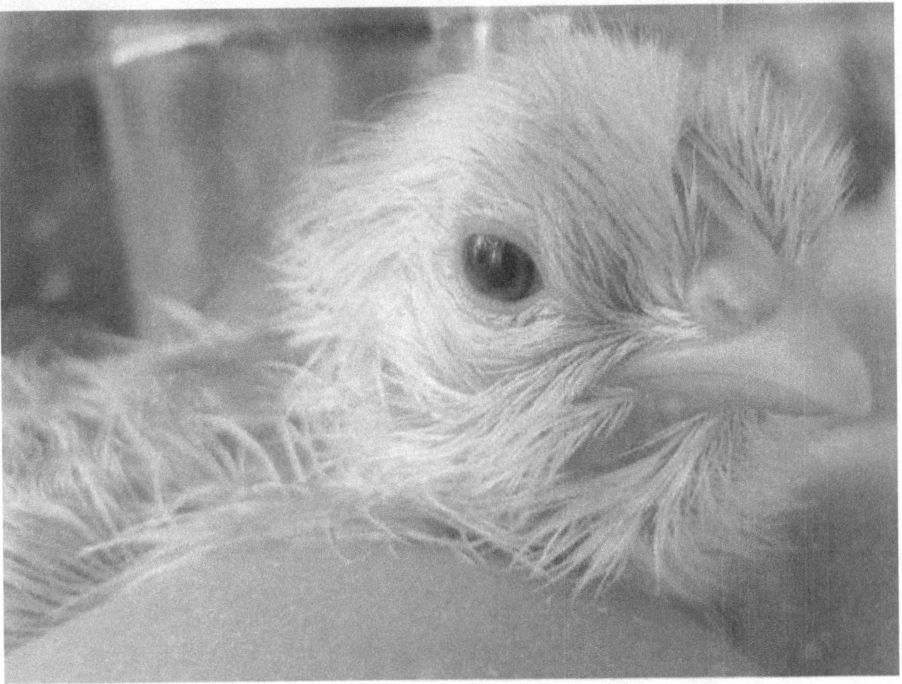

This book walks you through perfecting the incubating and hatching process so you can enjoy the exhilaration of the hatch without the angst of (many) dead chicks. I'm not an expert on incubation, having only tried my hand at it six or seven times, but luckily the difference between a 15% hatch and an 85% hatch is pretty easy for even the amateur to grasp. Follow the tips in this book and you'll soon have happy, healthy, homegrown chicks pecking through the clover in your backyard.

Why incubate?

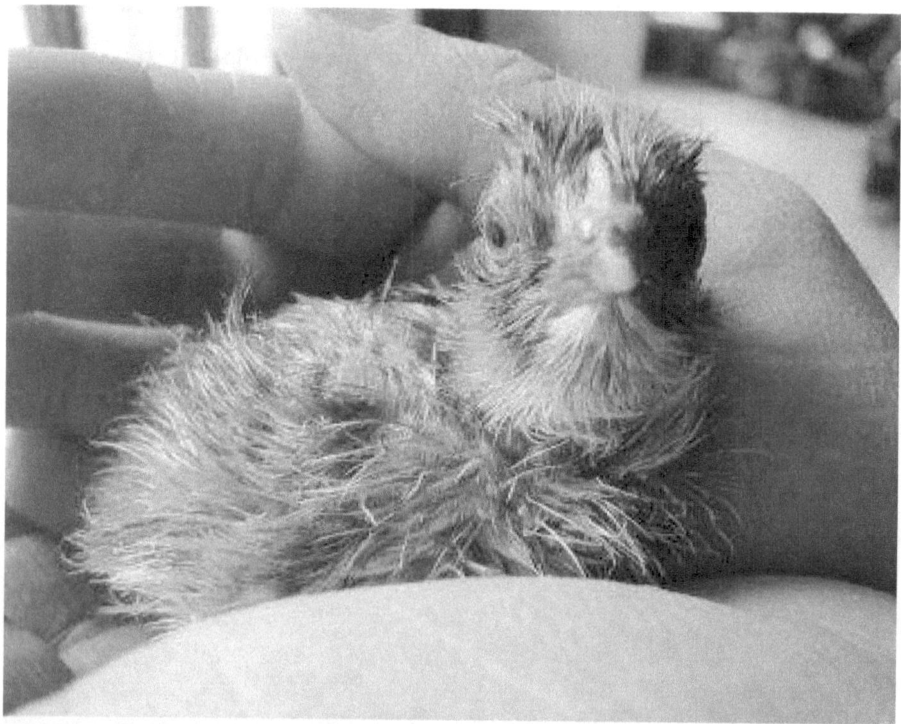

While we'd love our favorite hens to stick around forever, chickens have a limited shelf life. A hen begins to lay when she's about six months old, and she does her best work by the time she's a year and a half old. Depending on how hard-nosed you are, you might keep your laying hens for one year, two years, or three years, but after that, you're feeding large amounts of grain to an animal who has basically become a pet.

If you want to replace those old hens who are no longer laying enough to pay for their feed, you've got several options. You might be able to find someone local who is selling point-of-lay hens (pullets just beginning to churn out eggs). More likely, you'll order chicks from a hatchery.

There is a third option, however — incubating your own chicks from homegrown eggs. Raising new members of your flock at home has several advantages, the first of which is that you can incubate as few or as many eggs as you want. In contrast, hatchery-raised chicks usually require a minimum order of 25 birds to ensure that the youngsters produce enough body heat to survive two or three days in a mail truck. Backyard chicken keepers will be hard-pressed to find room for such a large flock.

Even more important from a permaculture point of view is the ability of the incubating homesteader to tweak the genetics of her flock. Hatcheries that sell to the general public focus first on breeding birds well suited to surviving in a hatchery setting, often aiming for appearance as the second priority. If you want to breed a bird that's able to hunt for its own food, you'll be much happier if you select your best birds and raise their young to become your next generation.

A final point in favor of incubating your own chicks is that you're the one in control of the process from start to finish. You don't risk diseases from the hatchery or someone else's farm coming along for the ride. Your chickens won't have to deal with the trauma of being shut up in a box or cage for an hour or two days as they make their way to your homestead. And you can start chicks at whatever time of the year matches your schedule.

Plus, you get to enjoy the Lifetime Channel version of Chicken TV—the miracle of new chicks pushing their way out of their shells.

The mother hen option

This book walks you through hatching chicks using an incubator, but there is an even better option—the broody hen. Until the twentieth century, even large chicken operations let mother hens raise chicks the natural way. However, industrial chicken keepers eventually decided that it wasn't worth fighting the broody instincts of hens who wanted to sit on the nest when the farmers wanted those hens to be laying eggs, so hatcheries bred broodiness out of many types of chickens. As a result, most chickens now available in the United States won't sit on a nest and raise chicks.

My long-term goal is to raise most of our homestead's chicks using a broody hen, but our experiments have met with mixed results so far. When we were able to get a hen to go broody, we loved the way she did all the work for us. She led the chicks out on pasture to forage for worms within a day or two, protecting her offspring from predators with her sharp beak. The little balls of fluff learned to eat Japanese Beetles and other scary-looking but delicious treats much faster than motherless hens did, and they managed to follow Mama to a perch two feet above the ground when they barely had wing feathers. I was also able to integrate the mother hen and her offspring into the main flock without worrying about the chicks starving since she chased everyone else (including the rooster) away from the feed until her chicks were well fed.

One slight downside to raising chicks with a broody hen is the price tag. You have to feed a broody hen for three or four months while getting no eggs in return—an estimated feed cost of $10.50 per hatch compared to about $2 in power for an electric incubator and energy-efficient brooder. Meanwhile, broody varieties tend to be less efficient at their other job of making eggs, so you're spending more on every egg the mother hen produces during the down season. That said, once you add in the lower feed cost for raising chicks that are better foragers and survive to adulthood more often, you might break even.

The real reason we're not raising all of our chicks with broody hens is that our chickens won't cooperate. Our White Cochin hen used to go broody at very erratic times of the year, so she was retired from the job. We're currently trying out Cuckoo Marans in hopes they'll be more willing to commit to a spring hatch. If that fails, our next attempt will probably focus on English Game Hens or Silkies, both of which are reported to have extremely well-developed mothering instincts.

All of this is a long way of saying that I can't tell you how to raise chicks with a broody hen. However, I can point you in the right direction to find more information. Harvey Ussery's The Small-Scale Poultry Flock includes a very handy chapter on raising chicks with a broody hen, and I highly recommend the book if your birds are more cooperative in the brooding department than mine are. If not, keep reading and learn how to hatch chicks yourself using an incubator!

Incubation basics

There are lots of techniques you can use to make your incubation experiment more successful, but the process really comes down to two numbers—21 days and 99.5 degrees Fahrenheit (37.5 degrees Celsius).

Incubation periods of common poultry

Chicken: 21

Duck: 28

Goose: 28-32

Guinea: 26-28

Muscovy: 33-37

Peafowl: 28

Pigeon: 16-18

Turkey: 28

Quail (bobwhite): 23

Quail (Japanese): 17-18

As you can see from the data above, chickens have an incubation period of 21 days, but what does that mean? You count the incubation period from the time you put the eggs in the incubator until the first chick pops out of its shell. So, if you want your chicks to hatch on a Saturday morning, you should set up your incubator on a Saturday morning three weeks prior to the hatch day. This is an important point because most beginning incubationists (like me) will stay up all night or skip work in the excitement of watching chicks pop out of their shells, so it's handy to plan the hatch for waking hours during your time off. Keep in mind that once chicks start hatching, it can take anywhere from 12 hours to three days for all of the chicks to emerge, which is why I recommend starting your eggs first thing in the morning.

The other essential factor to consider is temperature. There are two incubator heating methods (more on that in a later chapter), and the optimal incubation temperature will depend on the design of the unit. Incubators that use fans to circulate air should keep the temperature between 99 and 100 degrees Fahrenheit, while still-air incubators should be set to 102 to 103 degrees (as read at the top of the eggs). Most types of domesticated fowl are incubated at the same temperature, so you could put a duck egg in the incubator with your chicken eggs. However, be sure to do a bit of extra research to check the recommended humidity levels and exact incubation period if you're raising something other than a chicken.

While I'm throwing around incubation numbers, this is also the time to count your chickens before they hatch. Unless you get much luckier than I did, every one of your eggs won't turn into a chick. That means you might place two dozen eggs in the incubator if you want one dozen chicks.

Hatch rates for homegrown eggs (with no power outages or other problems) average 75% to 80%, while hatch rates for mail-ordered eggs are usually around 50%. When I knew very little of the information in this book, my first hatch rate was a measly 14%. This figure increased to 58% after a couple of tries with mail-order eggs and finally reached 86% with homegrown eggs. Hatch rates with broody hens tend to average 45% to

65%, with good mothers doing a better job and worse mothers hatching fewer eggs.

Choosing eggs

If you want a perfect hatch, you need to start with perfect eggs. Factors that influence an egg's hatchability include whether the egg was fertilized, in good shape, and how it was stored. In this chapter, I'll also explain how to buy and manage mail-order eggs and how to keep notes on individual eggs.

Seasons and parentage

Now that you understand the basics of why and how to incubate your own eggs, I'll start at the beginning and walk you through the entire process. The first step is to find eggs to put in your incubator.

The time of year deserves consideration as you plan your hatch. I prefer to incubate in February and March so the chicks are out on pasture during the peak grass-growing season of March through June. Then I start another batch in late summer to take advantage of the secondary pasture peak in September through November.

If you're revitalizing your laying flock, it's important to have chicks out of the shell by early to mid-April to ensure they are old enough to lay before days shorten in the fall. Otherwise, you'll be feeding non-laying pullets all winter.

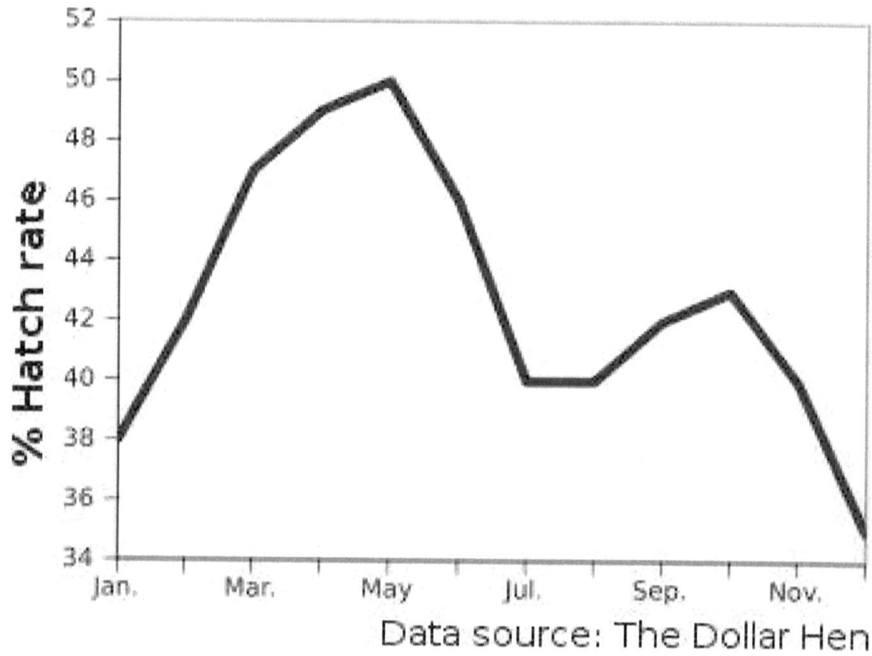

However, chicken biology dictates a slightly different hatch pattern. As you can see in the chart above, eggs tend to be most fertile in March through June, with a secondary peak in fertility in September and October. Don't feel obliged to follow the chart's lead, but do be aware that your results won't be quite as good if you're trying to raise chicks in the dead of winter.

A related issue is the health of the eggs' parents. Older poultry manuals admonish you to keep your breeding stock out on lush pasture, since the high-nutrition forage results in eggs that are more likely to hatch. In my own experience, I've found that breeds of chickens that produce brighter yolked eggs (meaning that the hens ate more bugs and greenery) have higher hatch rates.

Parent age is also a factor in hatch rates. Hens and roosters who have just become sexually active or who are more than two years old will produce fewer fertile eggs. I once tried to hatch eggs from four-year-old hens and had abysmal results, convincing me that even if these hens are still laying, most of the embryos aren't viable enough to mature.

Of course, you need to have a rooster if you want chicks (even though a hen will lay unfertilized eggs when no males are around). Some chicken keepers report issues with their roosters not mating frequently enough to ensure that all eggs are fertilized, but I've never had that problem. On the other hand, I keep fewer hens than the recommended dozen per rooster, so my flock's patriarch doesn't have to work too hard to do his job.

Inbreeding is a more tricky issue for the backyard chicken keeper. You may need to trade roosters with like-minded friends each year or buy a round of straight-run chicks to raise a new rooster annually, ensuring that your hens aren't mating with their brothers or fathers. Inbreeding tends to lead to lower hatch rates and a higher proportion of sick chicks out of the eggs that do hatch.

Egg shape and shell quality

Even if you've timed your hatch properly and have taken care with their parentage, there's still more to consider when selecting eggs to go in the incubator. If you can help it, try not to include eggs that are much larger or smaller than average for your flock, or those that are dirty, oddly shaped, or porous. Cracked eggs should definitely be discarded.

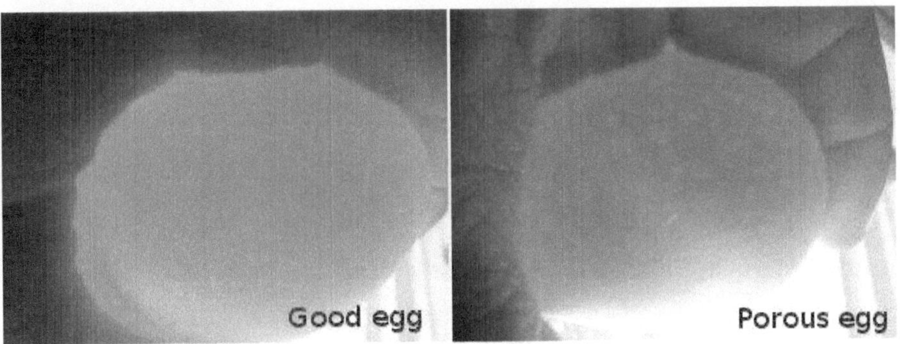

Once you get an eye for it, you can tell that the shell of an egg is a bit thin (porous) by noticing very slight gray blotches scattered across its surface. If in doubt, hold the egg up to a bright light—good eggs will be a solid color while porous eggs will be blotchy.

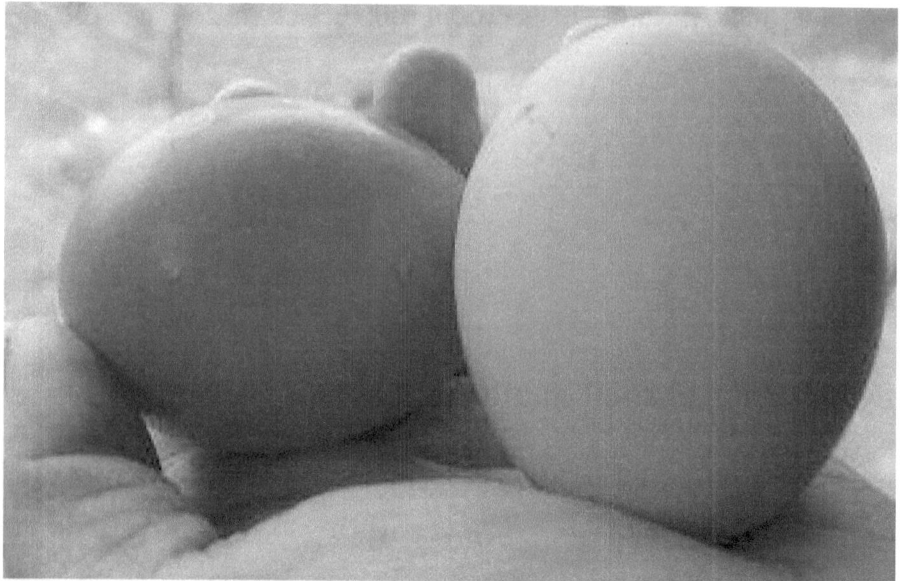

Despite the old wives' tale that round eggs will hatch into roosters and pointed eggs into hens (or vice versa, depending on who you're talking to), the shape of the eggshell has no effect on the sex of the chick.

It probably goes without saying that about half of your eggs are going to turn into girls and half into boys. If you're squeamish about slaughtering roosters, this may be a reason to stick to ordering sexed chicks from a hatchery. But if you do that, be aware that nearly all hatcheries euthanize unwanted male chicks. So you're merely outsourcing the necessary evil.

Dirty eggs can be cleaned using a special egg-washing solution you buy from hatching supply companies, but a better choice is to make sure that nest boxes are full of fresh straw and that you collect eggs twice per day so that washing isn't necessary. Freshly laid eggs are coated in a protective bloom that keeps out bacteria and makes the egg more likely to hatch, so you shouldn't wash a dirty egg in soap and water if you want the embryo to survive.

Storing eggs

Unless you have a large flock and can fill your incubator from a single day's laying, you'll need to store your eggs while you're in the process of gathering enough. Whatever you do, don't put these eggs in the refrigerator, since cold can harm embryos and make the eggs much less likely to hatch.

Instead, cut the top off an egg carton and put each egg in pointed-side down, placing the stored eggs in a cool (55 to 68 degrees Fahrenheit) place out of direct sunlight. To ensure that the embryo doesn't stick to the shell, put a thick book or a block of wood under one end of the egg carton and swap the carton end-to-end twice a day, tilting all of the eggs at once without touching them. The less you touch your eggs, the more likely they are to hatch.

Each day an egg waits to go in the incubator, it becomes slightly less viable.

The aging process accelerates drastically after day seven. In addition, high heat during the storage period can age eggs prematurely. For these reasons, try to get your eggs into the incubator within a week after they're laid and store them at or below room temperature.

Marking and final egg selection

I like to pencil a number on the blunt end of each of my eggs after collecting them. I keep a spreadsheet for each hatch telling the date the egg was laid and the likely identity of the mother (which I can tell from egg color and size). Later, I note down the location where the egg was placed in the incubator, when the egg pipped, and when it hatched. This note-keeping allows me to tweak my hatch process, revealing which breeds of chickens have more fertile eggs and which locations in the incubator might get too hot or too cold.

Although eggs will sit in the incubator vertically, I like to lay them out flat on the tray while choosing my best eggs. That way, I can make sure there will be room for each egg to lay down when the time comes for them to hatch.

This is my second chance to remove any eggs I've missed that are dirty or otherwise problematic. It's usually better to collect one more day's worth of eggs from the coop than to place a poop-smeared egg in the hot, humid environment of the incubator.

Buying hatching eggs

If you want to try your hand at incubation but don't have homegrown eggs, you can buy hatching eggs on the internet. This option is especially helpful for finding eggs of a less common variety. You might also be able to hunt down eggs from a flock that has traits you especially want, like a high percentage of broodiness or an ability to forage well on pasture.

That said, buying hatching eggs is pricey. I've spent anywhere from $1.75 to $2.08 per egg (counting shipping), and the hatch rate on these eggs was close to 50%.

On the plus side, you get more control over parentage with hatching eggs than you would when buying eggs from a hatchery. So mail-order eggs might make sense when selecting breeding hens for a serious flock.

Also, keep in mind that you can often buy just a few hatching eggs at a time. This allows you to raise an unrelated rooster to prevent inbreeding in your flock, or to try just one or two hens of a new breed.

Since you'll probably be looking for specific traits in your chickens, I can't tell you the perfect source for mail-order eggs. My first choice would be to google "Black Australorp hatching eggs" (or whatever breed you're looking for). You should also definitely drop by the "buy-sell-trade" section of the Backyard Chickens Forum (www.backyardchickens.com/f/67/buy-sell-trade).

You'll probably find several different options, so you'll need to decide which factors matter the most to you. When I was building a new flock using hatching eggs, I figured that price was less important than the photos of the parent birds, and was won over by a small farm that raised chickens on pasture. A source closer to you is likely to have chickens better suited to your climate, and shipping will also be faster, increasing your hatch rates. Buying hatching eggs is all about having more control over the new members of your flock, so let yourself be choosy.

Your eggs should arrive carefully packaged, often with an extra egg or two in the box to make up for any that were cracked during shipment. This is rare, however. In my limited experience, only one egg out of 46 arrived damaged.

Unpack your eggs immediately, arrange them in the incubator big end up, and allow the eggs to settle for at least twelve hours before beginning incubation. After that, you can treat your hatching eggs like any others.

Incubators

I haven't tried every incubator on the market (far from it), but I have experimented with each of the three main types available to backyard hobbyists.

If you live in a climate-controlled house and are willing to check on the incubator multiple times a day, you might have good results with a styrofoam still-air incubator from your local feed store. At the other extreme, if you live in a trailer heated by a wood stove (like we do), you'll need a high quality digital incubator.

The average American probably lies between the two extremes and might get by with a small digital incubator. I'll describe each option in more depth below.

Still-air incubators

Photo credit: Alex Ford from Raleigh, NC, USA, CC BY 2.0 <https://creativecommons.org/licenses/by/2.0>, via Wikimedia Commons

The cheap styrofoam incubators you can pick up at the local feed store might hatch chicks... if you have a room that varies in temperature by only a few degrees during the entire incubation period and are willing to monitor the incubator carefully. In that type of situation, some advanced incubationists have even managed to rig homemade incubators out of heat lamps, aquariums, and other components. Both of these types of incubators are described as "still-air incubators", meaning that there is no fan inside to move air around, distributing heat throughout the unit.

The cheapest incubator I tried out was a Little Giant Still Air Incubator complete with egg turner, which cost about $130 in 2024. I never had a single egg hatch with it because our mobile home isn't well enough insulated to keep the incubation temperature within reasonable bounds in such a cheap unit.

The trouble with this type of incubator is that its thermostat doesn't respond to changes in ambient temperature, so the incubator is only effective in a climate-controlled room. Reports on the internet do suggest, however, that if you have central heating/cooling and don't mind fiddling with the temperature dial a few times a day, you might be able to use this type of cheap incubator with good results.

Small digital incubators

Small digital incubators often have beautiful observation windows and are marketed as a good way to let children watch eggs hatch in the classroom. They are the lower-end version of what's known as a "forced-air incubator" since they use a fan to equalize temperature and humidity throughout the interior. These small units generally also have a computerized ability to maintain temperature (and sometimes humidity) inside.

The unit we tested was a Brinsea Mini Advance ($250 in 2024 dollars), which maintains a constant temperature quite well as long as the room the incubator is in doesn't have temperature swings of more than about twenty degrees Fahrenheit. It also includes an alarm to let you know if the incubator isn't able to keep up with external heat or cold. Additional features include an automatic egg turner and the ability to adjust several features using the digital keypad.

The trouble with these incubators is that they can be difficult to manage (although not as tricky as the styrofoam still-air incubators) since their small size makes them less insulated from outside conditions. In the worst-case scenario, a novice may end up getting a perfect view of chicks dying rather than hatching. If I were

going to use a model like this with kids, I'd make sure I performed a test hatch first and knew what I was doing before sharing the second hatch with soft-hearted children.

Unfortunately, there are a few disadvantages of the Mini Advance that you should be aware of. First, the incubator has a small capacity, holding only seven chicken eggs (which means that a good hatch from mail-order eggs might only yield three chicks). In addition, the eggs are incubated horizontally, which makes chicks more likely to develop in the wrong direction and get stuck during the hatching stage. We also discovered that this model beeps right before turning the eggs, which makes it tough to sleep with the incubator nearby.

The real Achilles heel of the Brinsea Mini Advance, however, is humidity. Not only does the incubator not monitor humidity (unless you buy the Mini Advance EX for twice the cash), but removing the large lid also results in extreme humidity swings around the eggs. I think that our very low hatch rate with the Brinsea Mini Advance (14%!) was due in large part to excessive humidity that resulted from following the manufacturer's instructions, which involved keeping the unit well-filled with water during the beginning stages of the incubation period. If you're on a budget

and don't mind doing math, you could probably use the egg-weighing techniques I'll explain in the next chapter to get good results with this incubator.

Even though we ultimately decided to upgrade beyond this small incubator, we still find it helpful to have the unit on hand. If a chick looks weak coming out of the main incubator, we can pop it inside the little incubator and use the Mini Advance as an intensive care unit while we nurse the youngster back to health. In addition, when hatching in cold weather it's handy to have a separate incubator in which chicks can dry off without bothering their siblings still in the egg, and this device does the trick. Just be careful when closing the lid on wiggling chicks so you won't catch their toes in the crack!

We chose the Brinsea Mini Advance because it had the best reviews of all incubators in its class, but you can also try the R-Com Mini and the Chick-Bator, both of which are cheaper and hold fewer eggs. Keep in mind, however, that a three-egg incubator might only hatch one chick, who will be very lonely without any siblings to cuddle up to.

High-quality consumer-grade incubators

Unless you can afford commercial models, there are very few choices for quality incubators that solve the temperature and humidity problems mentioned above. The only high-quality, consumer-grade unit we've tried is the Brinsea Octagon 20 Advance, and I thoroughly recommend it. (Or, perhaps, the newest model, untried by us: the Brinsea Ovation, $342 in

2024.)

Given the price tag, the Octagon 20 (or Ovation) isn't something to buy on a whim, but ours managed to hatch healthy chicks despite the wide temperature and humidity variations in our trailer. If you put good eggs in the Octagon 20, it will spit out chicks with nearly no work on your part.

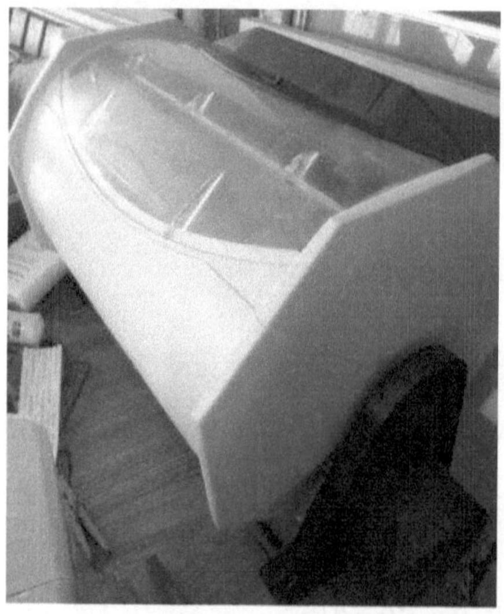

The Octagon 20 holds up to 24 chicken eggs, which is enough to ensure that you'll have several surviving chicks. You can place eggs into the incubator either horizontally or vertically, and the egg-turning cradle tilts the whole incubator without disturbing individual eggs. There's also no loud beeping and whirring, so this incubator didn't disturb my slumber.

The larger size of the incubator helps it maintain a more controlled temperature inside as well. Despite wide temperature swings outside the incubator, we didn't have a single low temperature alarm. However, we were forced to train a fan on the incubator during hot summer afternoons when our trailer's temperature exceeded 100 degrees.

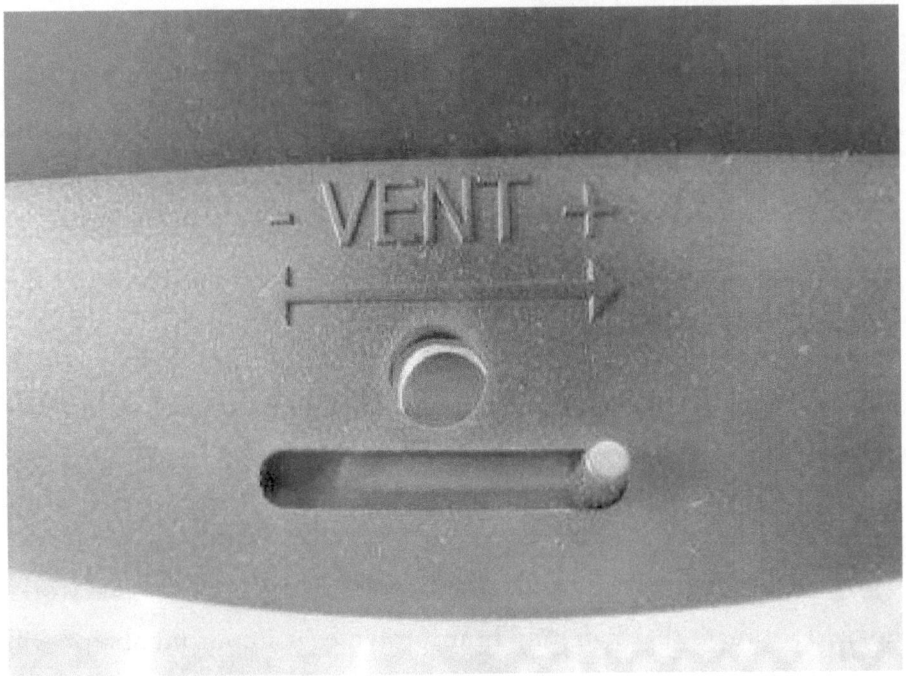

The combination of a digital humidity readout and an easy-to-operate vent makes it simple to keep internal humidity exactly where you want it. As I'll explain in a later chapter, it's also pretty easy to maintain high humidity during the hatch, even if you want to open the lid often to take out emerging chicks.

There are a few minor disadvantages to the Brinsea Octagon 20. First of all, since the egg-turning cradle moves the whole incubator from side to side, the unit takes up more space than you would expect, meaning that you can't place the incubator close to a wall.

Secondly, the egg turner plugs in separately, so you might accidentally unplug the turner without noticing. Taping both the incubator and turner to a power strip is a good quick fix to this issue, though.

Thirdly, there's a bit of assembly required (including installing the power cord), which will take about half an hour with a Phillips screwdriver. My egg-turning cradle also came missing a piece. This is probably an unusual occurrence, but it did mean that my first set of eggs had to sit around for an extra four days while the part was mailed to my farm.

Finally, if you're pushing the temperature envelope beyond what the manufacturers intended, you will see a slight decrease in the hatchability of eggs directly under the fan in the center of the unit.

Those slight disadvantages aside, the Brinsea Octagon 20 is a real workhorse! I estimate that hatching homegrown eggs in our incubator will equal the cost of ordering chicks from a hatchery in about ten hatches, after which our homegrown eggs will be essentially free. If you can afford it and want to incubate eggs, I can't recommend a better model, although you might check out some of the other incubators in its class.

The first 18 days

The decisions you make during the early incubation period have a strong effect on how many healthy chicks eventually pop out of their shells. This chapter covers deciding which way to align your eggs in the incubator, whether or not to candle your eggs, tips on turning the eggs, ways to keep the internal humidity at the proper level, and what to do if the power goes out.

Setting up your incubator

You've chosen your incubator and eggs, so it's time to start incubating! The instructions that came with your machine will help you set the temperature to 99.5 degrees for a forced-air model or 102 degrees for a still-air model, at which point it's a good idea to let the incubator run empty for a day while you monitor the temperature and humidity and ensure that everything is working properly. If there's any chance that someone in your household will accidentally unplug the incubator in the next three weeks, tape the cord into the electric socket as insurance.

The main choice you have to make at the beginning of the incubation process is how to arrange the eggs—either vertically, like they'd sit in an egg carton, or horizontally, the way they'd lie in a hen's nest. Although the latter option sounds more natural, in practice I've actually had slightly better results with vertical incubation.

As the embryo grows, the highest point in the shell becomes an air pocket which the chick will poke its beak into shortly before hatching. If this air pocket develops at the pointy end of the egg, the chick will find it difficult or impossible to hatch without help. Setting the eggs vertically with the blunt end up helps ensure that the chick will be situated the right way inside the shell.

If your incubator only allows you to lay your eggs horizontally, I wouldn't worry too much about it. That said, some incubationists set their eggs inside an egg carton with the top cut off to allow them to incubate vertically even in a simple incubator. More complicated incubators, like the Brinsea Octagon 20, often have removable dividers that let you choose how to align your eggs.

No matter how you arrange them, you don't want your eggs shifting and hitting each other. Egg turners that hold individual eggs make this point moot, but I find it helpful to add a piece of crumpled up paper in small gaps between less solidly touching eggs in our Brinsea Octagon 20 incubator. This ensures that I have room to lay all of the eggs flat on the tray during the hatch, but that the eggs don't roll against each other and risk cracking as the turning cradle rotates the incubator.

Egg turning

So what's the deal with turning eggs? In a nest, eggs get turned naturally as the hen shifts atop them, and this rotation is necessary to prevent embryos from sticking to the shell. If your incubator doesn't turn eggs automatically, you'll need to rotate the eggs yourself.

Eggs are usually laid flat in incubators that don't include an egg turner. To expedite turning, pencil an X on one side of each egg and an O on the other, then start with all of your eggs placed X-side up. Three or more times per day, open the lid of the incubator and quickly but gently rotate each egg 180 degrees so that the X has been replaced by an O (or vice versa).

The more often the egg is turned, the better. However, you also have to factor in the negative effects of cooling the eggs while the lid is off the incubator and of touching eggs with potentially germy fingers (even though you'll always be sure to wash and dry your hands carefully before turning). If you choose to turn your eggs more than three times per day, try to turn eggs an odd number of times so they sit on a different side each night.

If you can afford it, an automatic egg turner will definitely increase your hatch rate and decrease your stress levels. Most automatic egg turners are plug-and-play, but some will require you to select features like turning radius and number of turns per hour. The instructions that come with your incubator will suggest settings that work well.

Humidity and dry incubation

There is a lot of controversy among incubationists as to the perfect humidity for chicken eggs during the first 18 days. The instructions that came with my incubator recommended keeping internal humidity between 40% and 50% during the early incubation period. In contrast, followers of dry incubation prefer a much lower humidity, often between 25% and 35%.

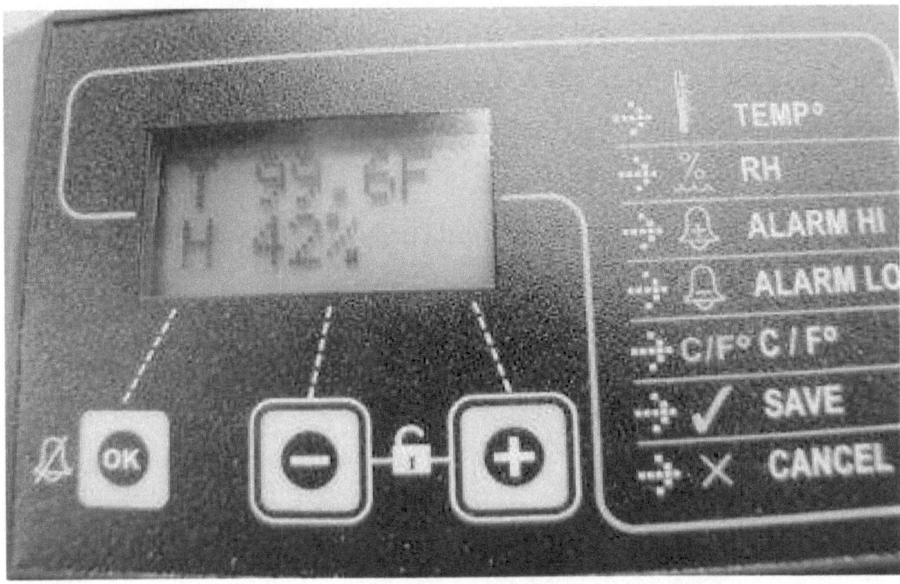

Before I delve into the intricacies of figuring out the proper incubator humidity, it's worth explaining how to change the humidity inside your incubator to suit your fancy. A few incubators have humidity pumps that automatically keep the internal humidity at a certain level—just program your choices into the digital display. For most incubators, though, you will have to manage the humidity manually using two or more wells (indentations) in the bottom of the unit, which you can fill with water to add moisture to the air.

The surface area of water, not the depth, will determine how much water evaporates into your incubator. So fill one well to any depth for a moderate amount of moisture and both wells to any depth for a lot of moisture. You can also open and close vents to manage the moisture, but developing chicks need as much oxygen as possible, so it's better to keep vents open and manage humidity using another method.

Now, to return to the controversy. As the embryo within an egg grows into a chick, the humidity in the surrounding air determines how much moisture leaks out through the shell. Escaping moisture makes the internal membrane that surrounds the chick shrink, creating an air pocket at the blunt end of the egg. Your chick will use this air pocket to breathe during the last few days before it hatches, so if the humidity in the incubator is too high and the air pocket doesn't develop properly, your chick could drown. At the other extreme, if the humidity is too low, your chick will dehydrate and die before hatching.

There are several ways to tell whether or not the air pocket in your egg is developing properly. One is to monitor weight loss (using a method I'll explain in the next section), aiming for each egg to lose 12 to 13.5% of its initial weight by day 18. Alternatively, you can hold eggs up to a light three times during the incubation process, drawing the location of the air pocket onto the side of the shell with a pencil each time. (The air pocket is visible as a paler region on the blunt end of the egg when viewed against a strong light.) The diagram on the next page shows the optimal size of the air pocket at 7, 14, and 18 days.

The final way to determine whether your eggs' air pockets are developing properly is to simply monitor the humidity levels within the incubator (assuming you've chosen a high-quality unit that tests for humidity). In my Brinsea Octagon 20, humidity readings between 25% and 35% result in just the right amount of weight loss for my eggs. During warm

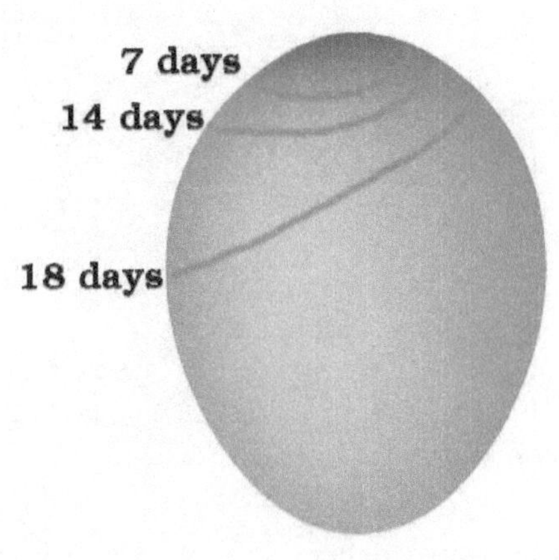

weather when the humidity in our southern mountains is high, I don't add any water to the wells of the incubator to maintain this internal humidity (true dry incubation), but I sometimes pour water into one well for part or all of the incubation period during the winter.

As you might expect, moisture management will vary depending on the humidity where you live and the amount of air that moves through your incubator. If you monitor weight loss carefully for a hatch or two, you should be able to correlate air-pocket development to humidity within the incubator and learn the best techniques for your region so you don't have to keep as careful notes during later hatches.

Measuring weight loss

The most accurate way of ensuring that the humidity levels within your incubator are on track is to weigh your eggs every other day between day 0 and day 18. While the math involved in egg weighing isn't complicated, it is time-consuming and repetitive. So I've provided a template spreadsheet at https://wetknee.com/incubating-and-hatching-homegrown-chicks to save you time and effort.

Note: Goal weight loss is for 13% at day 18

Day	Pounds	Ounces	Weight w/ tray	Tray w	Actual we	Actual v	Goal weight
0	3	3.7	3.23125	0.456	2.77525	0	0
2	3	3.1	3.19375	0.456	2.73775	0.0375	0.0400869
4	3	2.4	3.15	0.456	2.694	0.08125	0.0801739
6	3	2	3.125	0.456	2.669	0.10625	0.1202608
8	3	1.5	3.09375	0.456	2.63775	0.1375	0.1603478
10	3	1	3.0625	0.456	2.6065	0.16875	0.2004347
12	3	0.5	3.03125	0.456	2.57525	0.2	0.2405217
14	2	15.9	2.99375	0.456	2.53775	0.2375	0.2806086
16	2	15.4	2.9625	0.456	2.5065	0.26875	0.3206956
18	2	14.9	2.93125	0.456	2.47525	0.3	0.3607825

Actual percent weight loss at day 18: 10.8098

Note: Goal weight loss is for 13% at day 18

To use the spreadsheet, you'll just need to input the tray weight once (measured including the dividers and any crumpled-up paper spacers).

Then type in the weight of your tray with eggs every other day. As you can see in the screenshot above, the last two columns automatically calculate the actual weight loss of your eggs compared to the weight loss you were aiming for.

	A	B	C	D	E	F	G	H	I	J	K	L	M	N
	Day	Pounds	Ounces	Weight	Tray wei	Actual w	Actual w	Goal weight loss		Notes				
	0	3	4.1	3.25625	0.45	2.80625	0	0		Added water to one of reservoirs during day 1				
	2	3	3.3	3.20625	0.45	2.75625	0.05	0.04053						
	4	3	2.6	3.1625	0.45	2.7125	0.09375	0.08107						
	6	3	2	3.125	0.45	2.675	0.13125	0.1216		Refilled water in one reservoir this morning and				
	8			0	0.45	−0.45	3.25625	0.16214						
	10	3	0.8	3.05	0.45	2.6	0.20625	0.20267						
	12	3	0.1	3.00625	0.45	2.55625	0.25	0.24321						
	14	2	15.4	2.9625	0.45	2.5125	0.29375	0.28374						
	16			0	0.45	−0.45	3.25625	0.32428						
	18	2	14.1	2.88125	0.45	2.43125	0.375	0.36481						
				Actual percent weight los		13.3630								

The first example I've included was a summer hatch in which our ambient humidity was so high that even keeping both wells in the incubator completely dry for the first 18 days resulted in eggs that only lost 10.8% of their weight rather than the goal 13%. In contrast, during winter hatches (like the one shown on my second spreadsheet), I often notice that my eggs are losing too much weight.

There's not much you can do about eggs that don't lose enough weight (unless you add a dehumidifier to the room). But you can pour a bit of water into one incubator well if eggs are losing weight too fast. In my second example, you'll notice that I partially filled one of the wells twice during the incubation process to come out with a perfect 13% weight loss.

As you tweak humidity to keep the weight loss on track, remember that it's the *average* humidity over time that's important to your eggs, not the humidity at any given moment. In the spring, the humidity in my incubator may drop to 25% or a bit less during cool nights and then rise to nearly 40% on a hot day. (Temperature determines how much water the air can hold, thus affecting the humidity.) Your eggs won't mind losing a bit more weight one day and a bit less weight the next as long as the total weight loss ends up close to 13% of the eggs' initial weight at the end of day 18.

So don't stress out if you see a humidity spike within your incubator—only long-term humidity trends are problematic.

Calculating weight loss by hand

For my father (and anyone else who is scared to death of spreadsheets), here's how to do the weight loss math without a computer.

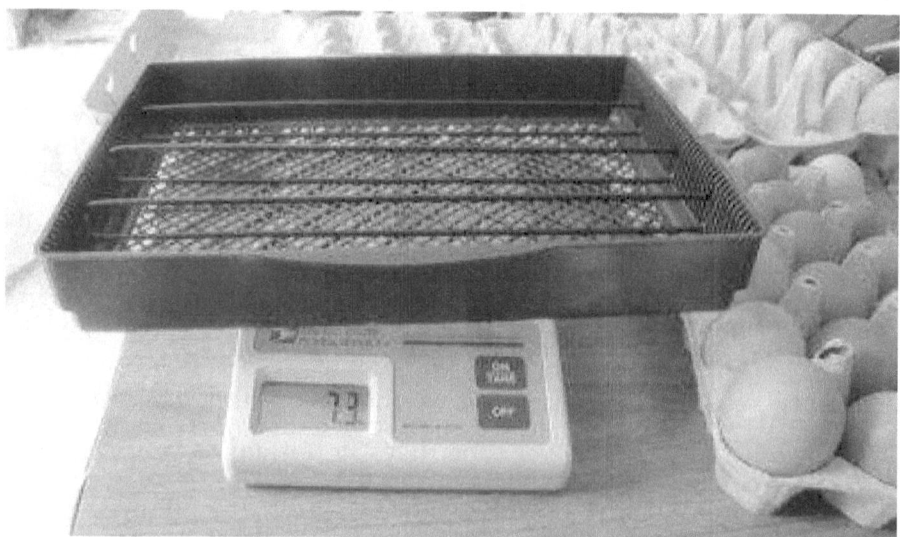

First, weigh the tray, dividers, and any crumpled-up paper you use as spacers and note that weight down in a notebook. This is the "Weight of tray" in the formulas below. If your incubator doesn't have a removable tray, you'll probably still want to put the eggs in something to allow you to weigh them all at once. The bowl, egg carton, or whatever container you use for this purpose will be the "tray" in your calculations.

Next, fill the tray up with eggs and weigh the filled tray to find your "Weight of eggs and tray." You should be starting this math on day 0 just before putting eggs in the incubator for the first time, at which point you can determine your eggs' current weight using the formula below:

(Current weight of eggs) = (Weight of eggs and tray) - (Weight of tray)

Our eggs and tray weighed 59.8 ounces at the beginning of our incubation period and the tray alone weighed 7.3 ounces, so the eggs weighed:

(Current weight of eggs) = 59.8 – 7.3

(Current weight of eggs) = 52.5

You can do this math using pounds, ounces, grams, or any other unit of weight. But if your scales spit out results in *both* pounds and ounces, you'll need to convert to one or the other. For example, my scale told me that the eggs and tray weighed 3 pounds 11.8 ounces, which I converted to 59.8 ounces.

The next step is to figure out how much I want the eggs to weigh at the end of the incubation period. We're aiming for a 13% weight loss, so:

(Goal weight at end of incubation) = (First day weight of eggs) X 0.87

For our eggs, that is:

(Goal weight at end of incubation) = 52.5 X 0.87

(Goal weight at end of incubation) = 45.7

It's also useful to know what our daily weight loss goal is:

$$\text{(Daily goal weight loss)} = ((\text{First day weight of eggs}) - (\text{Goal weight at end of incubation}))/18$$

$$\text{(Daily goal weight loss)} = (52.5 - 45.7)/18$$

$$\text{(Daily goal weight loss)} = 0.378$$

For those of you who never took algebra, be sure to do the subtraction before the division in the equation above. That's what the extra set of parentheses means.

Now I'm ready to find out if my eggs are on track with their goal weight loss on a certain day. After two full days of incubation, I weighed my eggs and tray again, subtracted out the weight of the tray, and got a new weight of 51.8 ounces. Did I have the humidity set right?

First, I calculated the goal weight loss for the day:

$$\text{(Goal weight loss on a certain day)} = (\text{Daily goal weight loss}) \times (\text{Days since incubation started})$$

$$\text{(Goal weight loss on day 2)} = 0.378 \times 2$$

$$\text{(Goal weight loss on day 2)} = 0.756$$

Next, I figured out how much the eggs should weigh now:

$$\text{(Goal weight on a certain day)} = (\text{First day weight of eggs}) - (\text{Goal weight loss on a certain day})$$

$$\text{(Goal weight on day 2)} = 52.5 - 0.756$$

$$\text{(Goal weight on day 2)} = 51.74$$

If you remember, my eggs weighed 51.8 ounces on day 2, so they might need to lose a hair (0.06 ounces) more weight, but they're close enough that I don't feel the need to adjust anything.

I hope this math doesn't look too daunting. Once you get over the long string of numbers, you'll realize that it's simple arithmetic, and will find that weighing your eggs every two days during incubation will increase your hatch rates. Here's a gratuitous cute chick photo to make it worth your while.

Candling eggs

Candling is a more common way of guessing what's going on in the incubator than monitoring weight loss, but is (arguably) less important and more potentially harmful. By holding eggs up to a strong light, you can tell as early as day eight whether your eggs are fertile and growing.

Unfortunately, the frequent handling (and heat from the strong light) can kill your delicate embryos, resulting in lower hatch rates than if you left the eggs alone. So why would you candle?

Large-scale hatcheries use the technique to allow them to take out infertile eggs and replace the duds with new eggs. This efficiency maximization is made possible by having a separate hatching incubator so that it doesn't matter if eggs in the main incubator encompass more than one stage of maturity. Please don't try this at home unless you have a similar incubator duo and the ability to brood chicks of multiple ages.

Backyard candlers argue that if you leave infertile eggs in the incubator for the entire three weeks, you risk having an egg explode and ruin the good eggs. However, I've never had a problem with exploding eggs and have noticed that when I autopsy dud eggs after 21 days, they haven't rotted enough to create the rotten egg effect. I suspect that as long as you put only fresh, uncracked eggs in the incubator, you don't need to worry.

That said, you might want to candle just to see what's going on inside the egg, or to figure out if a power outage killed your developing chicks. You can buy candling equipment or just use your hands (or a box with a hole cut in it) along with a strong LED light (other types of light are more likely to get hot and harm the egg).

Wait until it's completely dark (or go in a very dark room), then hold the flashlight under the egg and cup your hands so that no light leaks out around the edges of the egg. With white eggs, it's pretty easy to see what's inside. Brown eggs block more of the light, so you'll need to give your eyes a few seconds to adjust to the darkness. It can help to look at the egg out of the corner of your eye and rotate the egg gently until you can make out dark and light areas inside.

The easiest thing to see is the air pocket, a paler area at the blunt end of the egg. Between days six and eight, you will probably also be able to make out two dark blobs in the main part of the egg—the eye and the chick's body. These two blobs may look separate because the neck is thin and doesn't block the light very much. If you're hatching white eggs, you will probably also be able to see a network of veins radiating out from the chick, but don't worry if you can't make out veins in brown eggs.

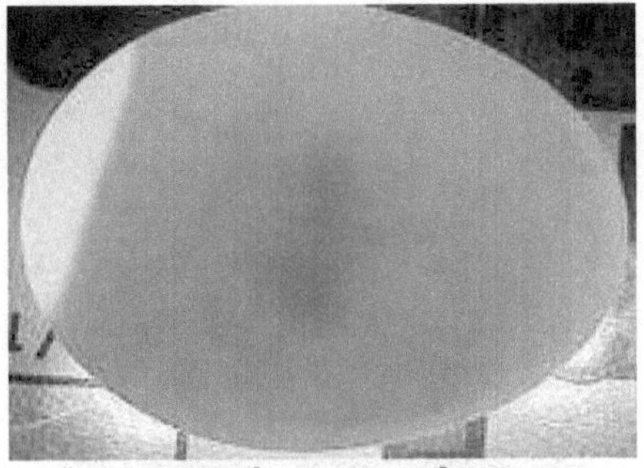

A good egg shows two dark spots at 6 days. The pale area at the blunt end is the air pocket. Light-shelled eggs allow you to see veins.

An infertile egg
looks clear.

Bad eggs can look very variable. Unfertilized eggs will be clear with no dark areas, while those that were fertile but died young will have blood spots, blood rings, or both.

Cloudy eggs that are uniformly dark inside except for the air pocket may mean that your egg died between day 10 and 16 (if you're candling later than day 8, of course). On the other hand, it can be tough to see inside brown eggs as the chicks get larger. So don't assume that just because it looks dark in there, your chick is dead.

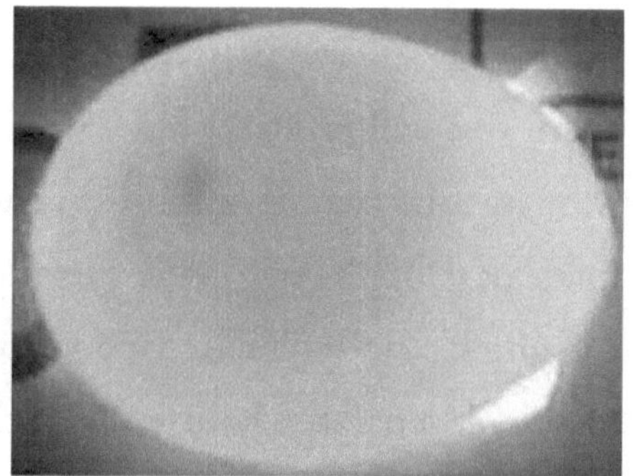

A ring is a sign of
a dead egg.

As a beginner, I wouldn't make any decisions based on my candling, but I would note down what I thought each egg was doing on my spreadsheet. When your eggs hatch (or when you autopsy the unhatched eggs on day 23), you can determine whether you guessed right during your candling day and you will be more confident next time.

Many thanks to Kelly from the now-defunct website http://shilala.hom estead.com/candling.html for sharing the photos in this section!

Temperature spikes and power outages

The last cause for concern during the first 18 days of incubation is temperature extremes. Your eggs might get chilled if your electricity goes out for more than half an hour, or if the room containing your incubator gets too cold for the heating element to keep up. At the other extreme, the temperature inside your incubator could exceed 100 (or 103 for a still-air incubator) if your room gets too hot. Your first goal should be to prevent these problems from occurring.

Even if you don't notice a spike high or low enough to set off your incubator's alarm, suboptimal temperatures are still going to affect your hatch. A slightly higher temperature may simply speed up the hatch by 5.4 hours per half degree Fahrenheit away from optimum, while a lower temperature will slow down the hatch. But you'll probably also find more chicks dead in their shells or perishing soon after hatching if you aren't keeping the temperature constant.

As the incubation temperature drifts further away from the optimal range, more and more chicks will die long before hatching. If your forced-air incubator reaches 105 degrees for half an hour, most of the chicks will probably die. So bring the temperature down as fast as possible once you notice a problem, especially if the chicks haven't been in the incubator long. (Eggs that have developed longer are slightly more able to handle high temperatures.) We've had good luck training a fan on the incubator during a hot summer day and are always careful to keep the eggs out of direct sunlight.

Cold temperatures aren't quite as likely to harm your developing chicks since mother hens naturally hop off the eggs for short periods every day.

However, the older your developing eggs get, the less they are able to handle cold temperatures.

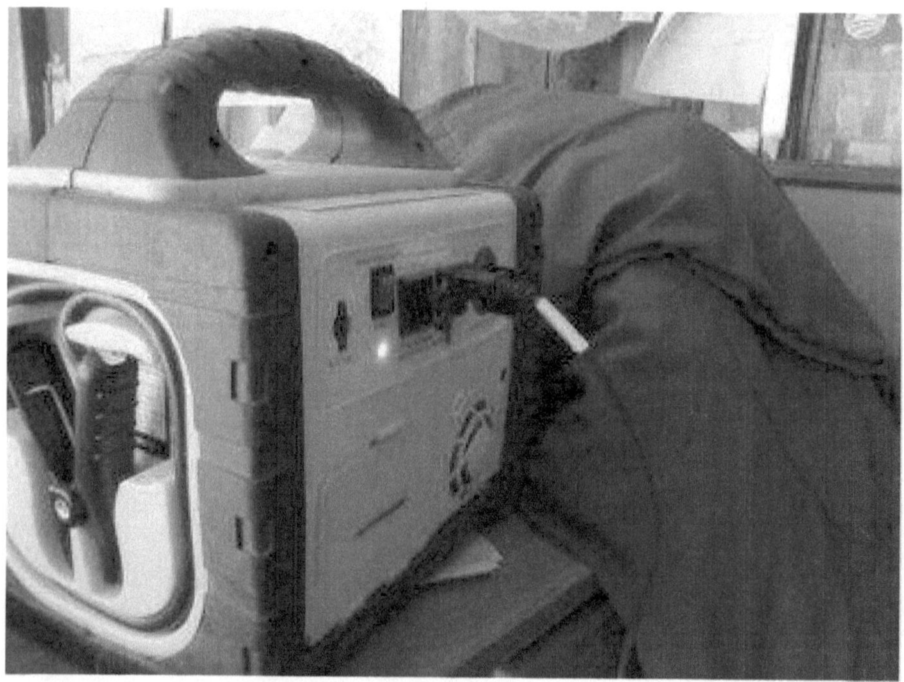

During power outages (the most common cause of temperature drops in the incubator), I close the vent and wrap the entire unit in a quilt. I also have a battery power pack that will run the incubator for a short time, so I plug in the incubator every half hour to bring it back up to the optimal temperature.

If you have a way of heating water, a hot-water bottle placed in the incubator can also help mitigate cold temperatures for a short time. However, if you live out in the sticks like we do and your power outage extends for several hours, you might have lost your eggs. Wait a few days, then candle to determine whether you'd be better off starting over.

Hatching

The most exciting part of the incubation process can also be the most traumatic if you don't know what you're doing. This chapter starts on day 18 when you prepare for the hatch, then walks you through helping chicks out of the shell and moving them to the brooder. Finally, you'll use a float test to determine whether late eggs are still good, will autopsy dead eggs to improve your hatch rate, and will clean the incubator.

Preparing for the hatch

You've waited patiently for 18 days and if you're lucky, nothing has marred the serenity of the humming incubator. Unless you candled your eggs, you may think that the absence of external activity equates to an absence of internal activity. But each chick is fully formed by day 18 and is ready to begin struggling out of the egg.

First, the chick breaks into the air pocket at the blunt end of the shell (at which time you may hear a muffled peeping from the incubator). Then the youngster will pip and unzip (as I described in detail in the introduction).

You should make some adjustments to the incubator on day 18 to make these coming struggles easier. The first step is to get the eggs into the proper position and stop turning them. Some incubators automatically shut off their egg turners at the appropriate time, but you'll need to manually remove the turner from others.

While you're at it, take out any dividers or egg cups and lay the eggs down flat on the tray, pointing the blunt ends toward the center, if possible. When chicks pop out of their eggs, the blunt ends hinge off like lids, and the first chicks will have an easier time struggling free if they're not pushing up against an unyielding surface.

Some sources recommend adding a sheet of paper underneath the eggs to make cleanup easier after the hatch. I used paper for my first hatch, but didn't think it did much good. It might even have been harmful since the paper was slick enough that chicks had trouble keeping their footing.

You'll want to clean the incubator tray well anyway after all of the chicks are out, so I'd skip the paper step unless the floor of your incubator is very slick. If you do add paper, use a paper towel or other item with enough texture to give your chicks a foothold.

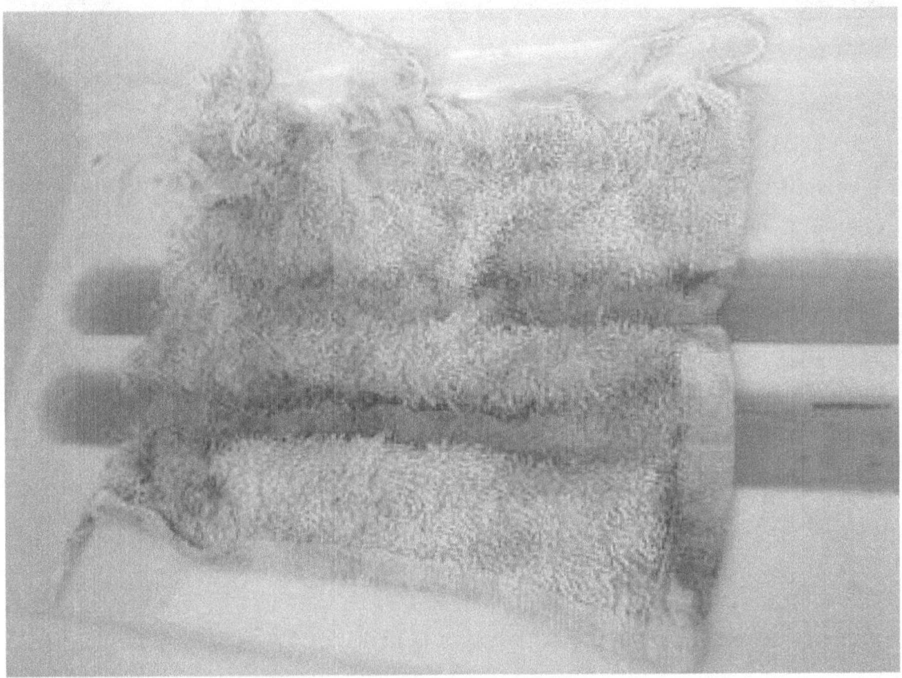

Increasing the humidity is very important, since the extra moisture lubricates your chicks as they wiggle their way out of the shell. Your humidity should reach or exceed 65% with the vent wide open, since struggling chicks use up a lot of oxygen and need fresh air.

To achieve that goal, first fill all of the wells in the bottom of the incubator with water. If the humidity still isn't high enough, take a clean rag or washcloth and drape it across the bottom of the incubator so that water wicks up from the wells to evaporate across a greater surface area. Incubator supply companies sell special evaporating card for a dollar or two apiece, but my reusable washcloths work just as well.

Depending on the design of your incubator, the wells may be underneath the tray or in the middle of the unit. If the wells are in a chick-accessible area, you will need to insert a chick guard (which will come with your incubator) to ensure that no chick falls into the wells and drowns while bumbling around in a stupor after hatching.

Day 18 is also a perfect time to get your brooder ready. (Turn to the last chapter for more information if you haven't raised chicks before). Although most chicks will hatch on day 21, early birds might pop out as soon as day 19. If you preheat the brooder 24 hours before the earliest chick could hatch, you'll have time to run to town and replace parts if something goes wrong.

Hatching and dry-off

You'll probably see at least one chick pipping (pecking the initial hole into its shell) on day 19 or 20. I like to record the date and time each egg pips to give me an indication of whether or not the youngsters are having trouble. I'll explain how and when to help chicks in the next section, but for now, just be aware that it's very normal to see a delay of 8 to 12 hours between pipping and unzipping (when the chick severs the blunt end of the shell and breaks its way free). On the other hand, if a chick has pipped but not begun to unzip 24 hours later, it might be in trouble. If you've done a good job with all of the early incubation steps, your chicks will probably pop right out of their shells one after another with no help from you.

Some manuals recommend leaving your chicks in the incubator for an entire day without lifting the lid to allow the youngsters to dry off completely, but I've had much better luck plucking chicks out of the incubator within 45 minutes of hatching and either plopping them into the brooder to finish drying off or placing them in a smaller incubator.

The trouble with leaving chicks in the incubator after they hatch is that the baby birds will stumble around madly, rolling eggs, and in the worst-case scenario, spearing partially hatched chicks with their claws. In my experience, newly hatched chicks are upset by not having anything soft to snuggle into, so they keep hopping around even though they're exhausted. Once I pop a newly hatched chick under our brooder, it stops peeping shrilly and soon falls asleep.

There are two downsides to removing chicks from the incubator one at a time throughout the hatch process. Firstly, chicks come out of the shell soaked to the skin and can easily catch a chill, especially if you're hatching in cold weather. Forty-five minutes in the incubator is just long enough that the chick's feathers are mostly dry, but is not long enough that they puff up into the protective ball of fuzz most of us think of when we envision a chick.

In warm weather (and even in cold weather if there are at least two or three other chicks in the brooder for the newly hatched youngster to snuggle into), this level of dry-off is enough. However, if your first chick comes out of the shell when your room temperature is below about 50 degrees Fahrenheit, you should either put up with the problems caused by leaving the chick in the main incubator until at least one more chick hatches and dries or should place the newly hatched chick in a spare incubator for a few hours. You'll be able to tell if you put a too-wet chick into a too-cold brooder because it will keep chirping frantically rather than quieting down after a minute or two.

The other issue with removing chicks from the incubator one by one is that every time you lift the lid, the incubator cools slightly and the humidity levels drop. You can counteract this problem to some extent with speed—open the lid with one hand while you snag the chick with the other. If it's pretty cold in the room, I like to heat up some water until it's steaming and top off the wells when I take off the incubator lid, since the hot water will keep the temperature in the incubator high and will also increase the humidity drastically.

Even though it's not 100% necessary, I open the lid a second time after the new chick is safely ensconced in the brooder, this time to tidy up the interior of the incubator. I remove large pieces of eggshell so chicks won't cut themselves on the sharp edges and I roll any disturbed eggs over so their pipping holes are facing up. (Sometimes, a chick will stumble across a neighboring egg and turn that chick face down, which makes it harder for the down-turned chick to hatch.) Finally, I quickly move eggs around so that the ones likely to hatch soonest have a little more open space around their blunt ends. As with removing the chick, I work quickly to ensure I don't lower the temperature and humidity in the incubator enough that it doesn't rebound a few minutes after I close the lid.

Helping chicks

As you can probably tell by now, I'm a very hands-on incubationist, so the advice in this section will fly in the face of conventional wisdom. However, as long as you keep the humidity and temperature at the right levels using the tips in the last section, you can be as hands-on as you want with no ill effect. In fact, helping chicks when they need it will increase your hatch rates and decrease your angst when a chick struggles and then perishes in the shell.

All of that said, I wouldn't recommend helping chicks out of the shell unless all of the following criteria apply to you:

You have some sort of critical-care unit prepared. Chicks you help out of the shell are likely to be weak and will need some extra time in a warm spot where they can't be picked on. A good critical-care unit is a spare incubator, already warmed up to the optimal temperature (99.5 degrees), but with the wells empty so the humidity is low. I like to place a few rags on the floor to make the chick more comfortable. This critical-care unit can double as your dry-off area during cold weather, and it's handy to put a buddy in with the troubled chick to keep the weakling calm.

You have a way of boosting the humidity in the incubator. As I mentioned in the last section, opening the lid frequently can harm chicks that are currently hatching. If you use my tips to keep temperature and humidity constant despite your intervention, this won't be a problem.

You're willing to cull chicks. The process of escaping the shell naturally kills chicks that are too weak or sick to make it in life. By helping chicks out of the shell, you're taking responsibility for euthanizing the ones that survive but are too damaged to live in your flock. I'll discuss how to cull chicks in a later chapter, but you should spend a minute now deciding whether you're willing to take a chick's life or whether you'd rather have the egg do it for you.

If all of these criteria apply to you, let's move on to when to help chicks. In most cases, an untroubled chick will pip (peck a hole in its shell) and then spend some time thinking about its options. After anywhere from a few minutes to a few hours, the chick starts hitting its beak against the shell in earnest to unzip itself, a process that usually only takes an hour or so once started.

You can tell the chick is having trouble if it gets stuck for several hours in the unzipping stage, either futilely banging its beak against the hole without making further openings in the shell or ends up mostly unzipped but unable to kick free. A chick is also troubled if it pipped but hasn't started unzipping after 12 to 24 hours, or if the bit of exposed membrane around the pipping hole is starting to turn tan and dry. Finally, if a chick somehow maneuvers itself so that it's trying to pip at the pointed end of the shell, it won't be able to get out, so you might as well help from the beginning.

If you have a stuck chick, how can you help? You'll need a basin of warm water at baby-bottle temperature, which is roughly 100 degrees Fahrenheit or 38 degrees Celsius. It should feel warm but not hot if dabbed on the inside of your wrist. You'll also need a clean rag and nimble fingers. It's best to find a warm spot for your surgery since you don't want the chick to be chilled before it hatches. Of course, you will have plucked the problematic egg out of the incubator and quickly reclosed the lid to make sure that everyone else stays toasty and moist.

The first step in the helping process is to moisten the egg's membrane, since it has probably dried out as the chick struggled to move past the pipping stage. Even if the humidity in your incubator is just right, a chick will eventually stick to the inside of its shell if it spends too long between pipping and unzipping. To rehydrate the membrane, dampen your rag in your bowl of warm water and encircle the egg in the wet cloth, then squeeze a few drops of water onto the exposed membrane around the pipping hole. Be careful not to drown the chick since its beak will be right there—you don't want any water to run into the egg; you just want to wet the membrane.

Since the chick has already started a hole, it should be pretty simple to gently pick off bits of shell and membrane, opening up a line around the shell just like the chick would have done. If your chick is ready to hatch, the membrane shouldn't bleed as you tear it. On the other hand, if you do see blood, don't panic—just stop immediately and return the chick to the incubator. A little bit of bleeding won't kill your chick. But if you keep prying the membrane apart too soon, the youngster will lose too much blood and perish.

Once you get the shell separated into two halves, your chick should be able to kick its way free. I hold the egg flat in the palm of my hand once the chick starts to struggle so that the chick can easily break loose. Sometimes I'll tilt the egg slightly (head end down) to help the chick slide out, but my experience has been that chicks who can't kick free when flat will have to be culled later.

Assuming your chick makes it out of the egg with your help, you'll want to pop it into the critical-care unit to dry off. Once the youngster is completely dry and moving around, transfer the chick to the brooder with its siblings, but keep an eye on it for a while. Perky chicks have an unfortunate tendency to drive less healthy flockmates out from under the brooder, pecking them viciously, so you may have to move the chick back to the critical-care unit (or cull it) if that occurs.

Be aware that it's normal for chicks you had to help (and even those who hatched naturally) to spend a lot of time sleeping for the first day or two in the brooder. If you don't hear frantic peeps, leave them alone and they'll be running around in a few days.

Chicks at end of day 22. Two aided chicks in top right are still sleeping it off, but have made it out of critical care.

Float test

One or two chicks might pop out of their shells on days 19 or 20, then you'll see a flurry of activity on day 21 and the beginning of day 22. If you have chicks that have pipped but not hatched by the beginning of day 22, check your notes to see if they've been working for more than 12 hours and decide whether or not to intervene.

But what about those eggs that haven't even been pipped? Are they duds?

You can use a float test to determine whether a living chick might still be inside pristine eggs, but I recommend waiting until day 23 (or until 24 hours after the last chick hatches if you had an extended hatch). Before you start, take a close look at the remaining eggs to make sure none of them has pipped or been cracked– if you do a float test on a pipped egg, the chick will drown. This test is mildly traumatic even to a chick inside an unpipped egg, so there's no reason to risk it until you're getting ready to toss the unhatched eggs.

Once you've confirmed that the eggs are uncracked and unpipped, fill a container with water that's roughly baby-bottle temperature, the same temperature water you used when helping chicks out of the shell. Wait until the water has stopped swirling around in the container, then take an egg out of the incubator and carefully lower it into the water with a spoon. If your egg sinks to the bottom, it was probably infertile from the beginning and is definitely a dud now. If it floats, take a careful look at the floating pattern:

Does the big end stick up above the water with the narrow end pointing straight down? If so, your egg is probably a "yolker" that was either a dud from the beginning or died young.

On the other hand, if your egg floats at more of an angle, almost horizontally, the chick might still be alive inside. If the egg starts to move around on its own or peeps, the chick is definitely alive. Carefully take the egg out of the water, wipe it dry, and pop it back into the incubator for another day or two.

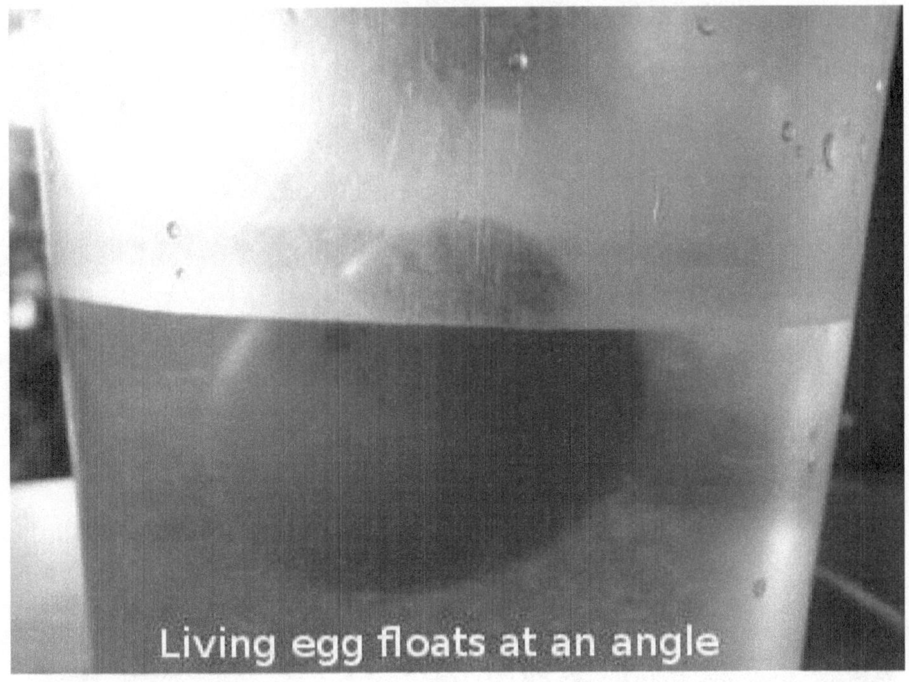

Egg autopsy

The least pleasant part of hatching is breaking apart the dud eggs afterward to determine what went wrong. Autopsying your eggs isn't essential, but it does help make you a better incubationist. If you know what killed your chicks, you can prevent the same problems from reoccurring in the next batch.

If your chick got all the way to the pipping stage, it's not necessary to autopsy the egg. You probably chose not to help a weak chick out of the shell, and it likely died either from sticking to the membrane (if the humidity wasn't high enough during hatch), due to genetic leg problems, or from pipping at the narrow end of the shell. Unless you're a pro, you

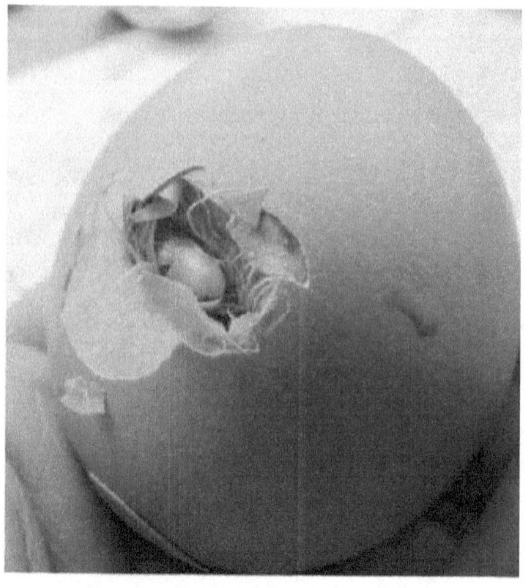

probably won't be able to tell the difference between the first two, and the last is obvious without cracking the shell.

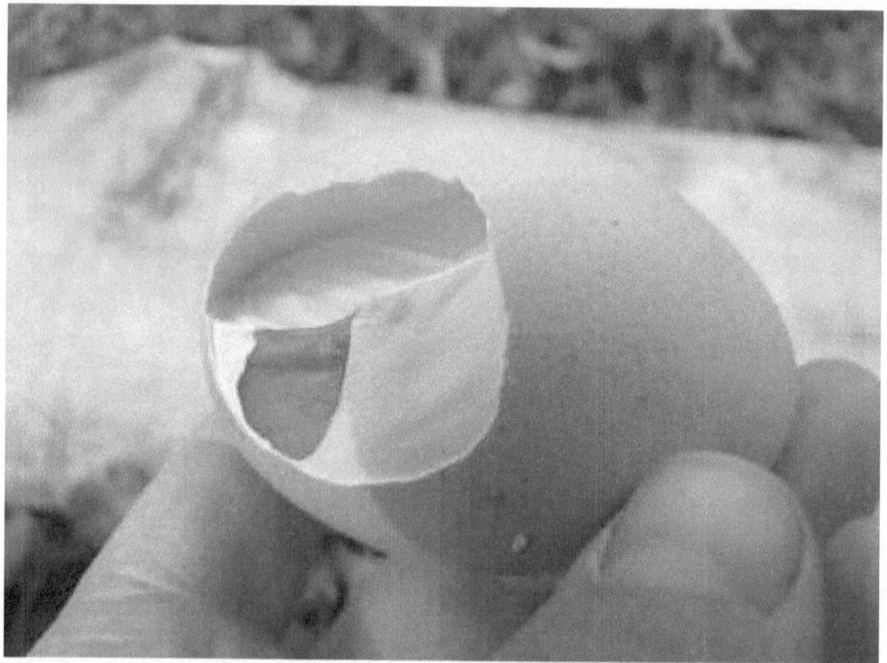

A partially formed chick that didn't break into the air pocket could have died from a variety of causes. These could be the result of improper humidity (often too high), or of temperature extremes late in the incubation period. I'll help you troubleshoot these problems in the next chapter.

A "yolker" is an egg that never developed at all (or at least, not enough that you can see the embryo with the naked eye). Yolkers could have been infertile from the beginning or might have been killed by temperature swings during the early part of the incubation process. If you get several yolkers and think the incubator did its job, you should consider the factors that influence egg fertility, listed in the "Choosing eggs" chapter. You should also expect a higher percentage of yolkers with mail-order eggs due to potential rough handling at the post office.

I'll delve further into problems that might cause chicks not to hatch in the next chapter, but for now, here's another cute chick photo to counteract the autopsy process.

Incubator cleanup

When you turn off your incubator at the end of the hatch, be sure to take a few extra minutes to sterilize it as much as possible. Some incubationists see declining hatch rates over time as germs build up in their equipment, but that's an easily preventable problem.

Fill up your sink with warm, soapy water plus a tablespoon or two of bleach, and soak any parts of the incubator that are solely made of plastic. Meanwhile, carefully wipe down the lid (or whichever portion contains the electronics) and set it out in the sun to dry. If you're using a Brinsea Octagon 20, or another incubator that includes insulation sandwiched between two layers of plastic, don't submerge that part of the incubator—wipe it down carefully just like you did with the lid. Now rinse the parts of the incubator that have been soaking and let them dry as well.

You can either throw away the rag you used to wick moisture out of the wells or toss it in your laundry basket to reuse after being cleaned. Ditto any rags that acted as bedding in your critical-care incubator. We're fans of reusables and have had no problem with disease buildup when using laundered rags more than once.

Incubation problems

The best way to learn to be a better incubationist is to spend an extra hour after all of your living chicks are safely in the brooder hunting down the causes of their siblings' demise. This chapter will cover reasons chicks might not survive to hatch, along with maladies that show up soon after the chick comes out of the egg.

Viability, hatch rate and survivability

The first thing to understand when troubleshooting your hatch is that some chicks are almost certainly going to die, either in the egg or soon thereafter. If you're doing a good job, most will grow up to be healthy chickens, but it's not worth beating yourself up about the few that don't make it.

So how can you tell the difference between a normal mortality rate and a problem you need to fix? I like to calculate the percent of viable eggs, the hatch rate, and the survivability of my chicks to get an idea of where issues might lie.

The percent of viable eggs is simply the number of eggs that showed some sign of life, meaning that they were fertilized and didn't die very young. To calculate your percent of viable eggs, autopsy or perform a float test to figure out how many of your duds were yolkers (see the last chapter), then use the formula below:

Percent viable eggs = ([(Total # eggs) - (# yolkers)] X 100%)/(Total # eggs)

For example, in my most recent hatch, two out of 21 eggs were yolkers, so 90% of my eggs were viable.

Hatch rate is just what it sounds like—the percentage of your chicks that made it out of the shell. This number doesn't take into account any losses you might see when weak chicks perish soon after hatching, and most incubationists also leave yolkers out of their calculations. So in the formula below, the number of viable eggs is how many eggs you put in the incubator that didn't turn out to be yolkers, and the number of unhatched eggs only includes those that showed some sign of development.

Hatch rate = ([(# viable eggs) - (# unhatched)) X 100%]/(# viable eggs)

In the same hatch mentioned above, I had 19 viable eggs, one of which developed partially but didn't hatch. So my hatch rate was 95%.

An easier way to calculate hatch rate is simply the percentage of eggs you put in the incubator that turned into living chicks. That type of hatch rate is what most folks mean when they refer to hatch rate, and is how I calculated the hatch rates in previous sections. However, this more complex version of hatch rate is helpful in troubleshooting incubation problems, so we'll use it for this chapter.

The third factor to consider is survivability, which refers to the percentage of your hatched chicks that live until their one-month birthday. The idea is that problems in the egg or incubator might show up as much as four weeks later, when weak chicks fail to thrive and finally kick the bucket.

In determining percent survivability, I usually don't count chicks lost to predators or anything else that's clearly not hatch-related. But I do count malformed chicks that have to be culled and chicks that keel over in the first week or two for no apparent reason.

Survivability = ([(# hatched chicks) - (# chicks dead by 4 weeks)] X 100%)/(# hatched chicks)

Out of the 18 chicks that popped out of the shell, I had one very late hatcher who died during the first week in the brooder, so my percent survivability was 94%.

Causes of incubation-related problems

So what do you do with the numbers you calculated in the last section? If you had a very good hatch in which the percent of viable eggs, hatch rate, and survivability of your chicks were all greater than 75% and were approximately equal to each other, you don't need to do anything. But if you see a disproportionately low number for one of these figures, it points you toward an error you can fix.

The dichotomous key below can help you pinpoint your problem. To read the key, start at the top and answer each question, skipping ahead as ordered until you find the most likely cause of your incubation issue.

1. Are your viability, hatch rate, and survivability all above 75%?

Yes—No need to troubleshoot. Good job!

No—go to 2

2. Did you begin with mail-order eggs and see a viability, hatch rate, and survivability above 50%?

Yes—No need to troubleshoot. Good job!

No (either your rates were lower or you didn't use mail order eggs)—go to 3

3. Were fewer than 75% of your eggs viable?

Yes—go to 4

No—go to 5

4. If possible, find more eggs from the same source and crack several of them open to test the eggs' fertility. Carefully separate the yolk from the white the same way you would when baking, pouring the contents from shell to shell until the white slips out into a bowl. Next, rotate the yolk (by passing it from one shell half to the other) until you can pick out the blastoderm—the living part of the egg, which is visible as a small, pale dot. Which of the photos and descriptions on the next page best matches your blastoderm?

If your blastoderm is a solid white circle like the one to the right, your egg is infertile. Infertile eggs are generally the rooster's fault. Your rooster could be shooting duds, could have too many ladies to please, or might be

ignoring certain hens in favor of his primary girlfriends. He may also be malnourished or old.

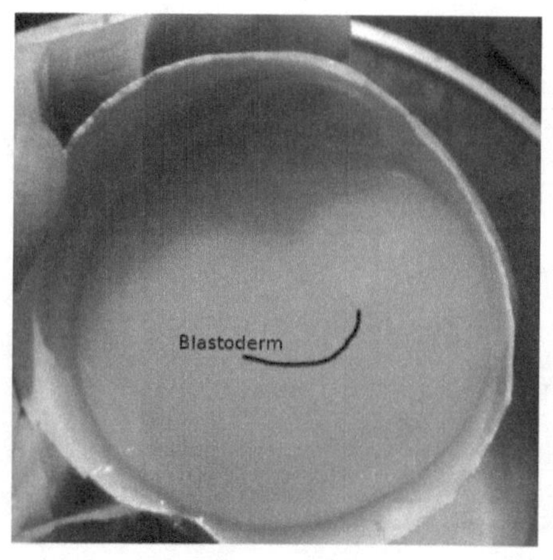

If your blastoderm is a light-colored bulls-eye, rather than a solid white circle, your egg is fertile. Egg management is usually the issue if all or most of the eggs you test show up as fertile, but you still find a lot of yolkers in your incubator after the hatch. Mail-order eggs often have a high percentage of yolkers due to rough

handling, but you can get the same effect by storing your eggs too long, using dirty eggs, letting eggs get too hot or cold during storage (below 55 or above 68), or incubating eggs from parents who are too closely related or are malnourished. If you live above 5,000 feet, you may have to expect a lower viability rate.

5. Did any embryos/young chicks die in the shell? (In other words, was your hatch rate low?)

Yes—go to 6

No—go to 11

6. When you performed your autopsy (see the last chapter), were the viable but dead-in-the-shell eggs fully formed? (Chicks in the shell look strange, but if they're fully formed, you'll see beaks, legs, eyes, and feathers, as in the photo to the right.)

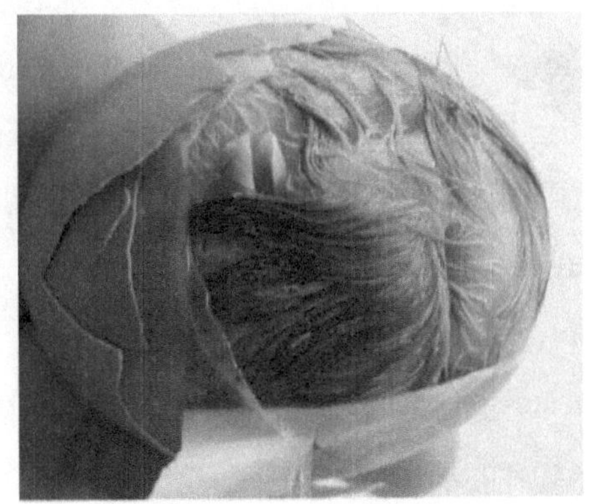

Yes—go to 7

No—A power outage or temperature spike is an obvious cause of partially developed chicks found dead in the shell, especially if they've all developed to about the same stage. Chicks that barely develop and die before they really look chick-like could also have been killed by improper incubator temperatures, not turning the eggs correctly, poor ventilation, or inbred, diseased, or malnourished parents. Skip to 9 if you'd like to determine whether temperature might be the culprit.

7. Did the dead chicks pip (break a hole in their shell)?

Yes—go to 8

No—got to 9

8. Did the chicks that later died pip at the large end of the shell?

Yes—The problem is probably insufficient humidity in the incubator during hatch, especially if you can tell that chicks are sticking to the insides of their shells. Be sure to raise the humidity to at least 65% at day 18 and consider only opening the lid once a day after chicks begin to pip. However, pipped chicks sticking to their shells could also be the result of excessive humidity or low temperature earlier in the incubation process, especially if the chicks that do hatch are too liberally smeared in albumen. A less common cause of chicks pipping at the large end of the shell but dying before they can hatch is insufficient ventilation—make sure the vents on your incubator are fully open during hatch. Weak chicks (due to a vitamin E deficiency) also often die at this stage, as do malformed chicks due to inbreeding or improper nutrition of the parent chickens. (See 12 and 13 below.)

No—Chicks that pip at the small end of the shell won't be able to break free without help. To prevent the problem in future hatches, incubate eggs vertically with the large end up. Consider helping any chicks that pip at the narrow end of the shell.

9. Of the chicks that hatched, did most or all come out of the shell within a 24-hour span centered around day 21?

Yes—go to 11

No—go to 10

10. Which of the following best describes your hatch?:

Most chicks hatched before day 21—High incubation temperatures or improper egg storage will often result in early chicks, some of which have bloody navels and are smaller than usual. Your incubator's thermostat might need to be checked, or you can simply set the unit to run a bit cooler next time. Alternatively, your room temperature might be the problem if you were incubating during the summer and the incubator overheated.

Most chicks hatched after day 21 or your hatch was elongated, spreading out over several days, with several flabby-looking (soft) chicks—Improper egg storage is a possibility. But if you didn't see corresponding low viability rates, the issue is probably low or irregular temperatures in the incubator. Make sure your room temperature wasn't too cold and that your incubator thermostat is properly adjusted. Excessive humidity during the first 18 days of incubation can also cause late-hatching, soft chicks.

11. Were there chicks that hatched but later died obviously malformed?

Yes—go to 12

No—Chicks that hatch but remain weak and die within a week or two could be the result of inbred, diseased, or malnourished parents. If you see low hatch rates along with lots of chicks dying soon after hatching, the problem may be improper incubator conditions weakening chicks as they develop.

12. Did the malformed chicks have leg or foot problems?

Yes—go to 13

No—Other than leg problems, the only other common malady that chicks show as soon as they pop out of the egg is wry neck. You'll notice chicks with wry neck because they have trouble staying upright, often ending up on their backs frantically trying to turn themselves over. When upright, these chicks tend to bend their heads back (especially when stressed) so their beaks are constantly pointing at the sky. Wry neck could be an injury sustained coming out of the shell, but if you see lots of chicks with wry neck, the culprit is more likely a vitamin deficiency (vitamin A or E or thiamine or manganese). See the next section for cures, and be sure to nourish the parent birds better before collecting eggs for your next hatch.

13. Which of the following best describes your chicks' maladies?

A. One or both feet have toes curled up and seemingly unable to straighten—Curled-toe paralysis can be caused by a riboflavin (vitamin B2) deficiency, inbreeding, or by low humidity in the incubator. If you see curled toes on only one foot, the culprit is likely to be an injury sustained as the chick fought its way out of the shell.

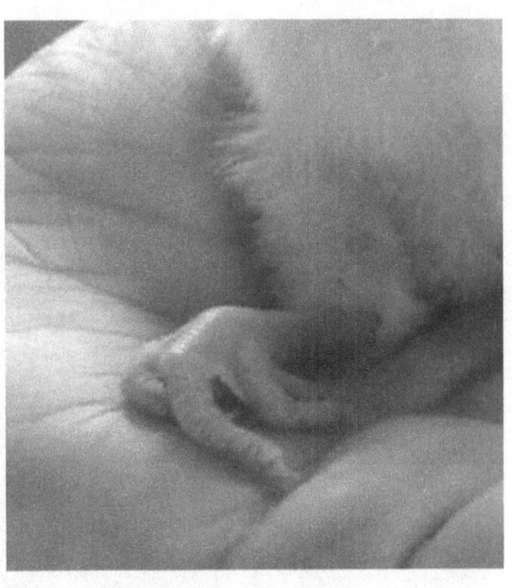

B. The chick appears to be doing a split with both legs out in opposite directions—Known as spraddle leg or splay leg, this condition is nearly always caused by a slippery surface in the incubator or brooder that led the chick to injure itself when it tried to stand up. Make the surface less slippery with appropriate bedding and you won't have any more spraddle leg chicks. Less common causes of spraddle leg include temperature swings in the incubator, vitamin deficiencies, trouble hatching (such as pipping at the wrong end of the egg), or overcrowding causing chicks to pile on top of each other in the brooder.

C. A single leg won't straighten—This problem is usually a slipped tendon, which can be caused by a diet deficient in manganese, choline, nicotic acid, pyridoxine, biotin, or folic acid, or by physical stress while getting out of the egg.

Caring for sick chicks

Problems that require treatment immediately after your chicks hatch include wry neck, spraddle leg, curled-toe paralysis, and slipped tendons. (See the previous section for descriptions of these leg, foot, and neck problems.) In addition, chicks that remain attached to some of their yolk when they hatch or that have bloody navels will need to be separated from the other chicks so their bellies don't get pecked at. Chicks that you help out of their shells will probably also need a little TLC before they're ready to join the flock.

In all of these cases, your first decision must be whether you want to try to save the chick or euthanize it. I'm tender-hearted, but I have limited patience with babying sick animals for days on end. So I walk a middle road and give sick chicks a day or two to bounce back, after which I cull any chicks that aren't obviously healed.

I've found that it's psychologically easier to cull a chick soon after it hatches compared to several weeks down the line when I realize the young chicken is half the size of its peers. I also don't want problematic birds to stay in the gene pool since that means I may continue to see the same problems in subsequent hatches. That said, there are times when just a day or two of warmth and/or isolation will allow a chick to bounce back and be as good as new.

The chicks I've had that hatched with wry neck recovered when I simply manhandled them to get their heads moderately straight, allowing me to slip them under my Brinsea Ecoglow brooder. Chicks that I helped out of the shell often get 12 to 24 hours in an isolation incubator to dry off thoroughly before being moved into the brooder with the rest of the chicks. In both cases, the trick is to help ungainly chicks get thoroughly warm—they might not be coordinated enough yet to figure out how to wiggle completely under the brooder, but if you help them, they'll go to sleep and often wake up healed.

If you think the problem is a nutrient deficiency, many incubationists recommend using a children's liquid vitamin (Enfamil Poly-Vi-Sol). They dose the chick with three drops a day for a week, then taper off the dosage so the chick is no longer taking vitamins by the end of the second week. Combine your medication with the physical therapy in the next paragraph for best results. If your chick has wry neck and hasn't recovered within a day or two, you will have to help the chick eat and will need to water the chick using an eyedropper several times a day if you want it to survive.

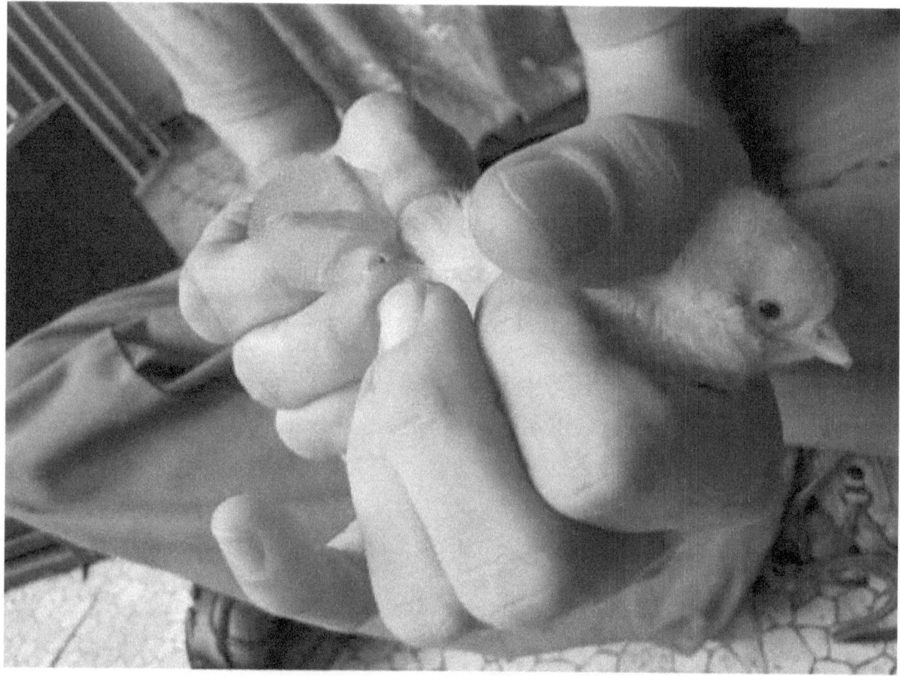

Chicks with leg or foot problems require more drastic action. Spraddle-leg chicks are the most likely to bounce back if treated immediately—make a hobble out of a band-aid, forcing the chick's legs back into the proper alignment. Curled toes can be straightened at least somewhat with a splint made out of a band-aid or transpore tape (as shown above). In both cases, you'll need to resplint the chick's feet or legs once or twice a day, and you'll have to watch to make sure the other chicks don't peck at the bandage and accidentally draw blood from the problem chick. Be sure to enlist someone to help you with the operation because chicks do not enjoy being restrained and manhandled.

A slipped tendon can sometimes be reset if you make the effort as soon as you notice the problem. You might be able to feel the tendon through the skin and pinch or push it back into place. However, the tendon will sometimes slip back out multiple times and you'll have to repeat the treatment.

In all cases, the trick to speedy recovery is speedy treatment. If you wait until a day after the chick has left the shell before trying to splint curled toes, you'll be much less successful. Similarly, if you put a chick with a bloody naval in the brooder and don't notice it being picked on for a few hours, it's likely to give up the ghost even after you isolate it.

Finally, don't feel too bad if the chick you aid ends up dying or having to be culled. Weak chicks that don't recover within a few days after treatment would be a drain on your flock, so their death by natural causes could be a blessing in disguise.

Culling chicks

If a chick hatched with a malformation you can't (or don't want to) correct, or if it's simply so weak it's being picked on by its siblings after a day in isolation, the kind thing to do is to put the animal out of its misery. But how?

After researching all of the options, I decided that the most humane (and quickest) method is to suffocate the chick using carbon dioxide. Although this sounds high-tech, you just need a sealable Tupperware container, a shorter container to fit inside, and some baking soda and vinegar.

You may have mixed baking soda and vinegar together to make an erupting "volcano" for an elementary school project, in which case you know that the duo foam up on contact, releasing carbon dioxide into the air. In terms of proportions, you'll want to perform a few experiments before killing your chick to find out how much baking soda and vinegar are needed to react well. I covered the bottom of my smaller reservoir with about half an inch of baking soda and poured on perhaps another inch and a half of vinegar to get the best foaming action without overflowing my inner reservoir. (No need to get the chick wet and uncomfortable during its last seconds.)

Now that you know what you're doing, prep your gas chamber by adding baking soda to the inner reservoir then putting the chick inside the larger container. Pour the vinegar on top of the baking soda and quickly close the lid on the entire chamber. In my experience, a chick will peep for about two seconds in the container before collapsing, then will spend perhaps another ten seconds twitching (during part of which it is probably already dead and is definitely unconscious). Leave the lid on the container for a few extra minutes to be sure, then bury your chick.

Although it's sad to have to cull a chick, in the end, it's kinder to remove the chick before its flockmates peck it to death. Try not to repeat my mistake of spending several days agonizing over the decision of whether and how to euthanize an ailing chick—get it over with now and enjoy the deceased's healthy siblings.

Raising chicks

Although this book isn't really about raising chicks, it seems a little cruel to leave you hanging with cute balls of fluff in your hands and no idea what to do with them. So this final chapter hits the highlights of chick care. But please do research further if you want to go beyond the basics.

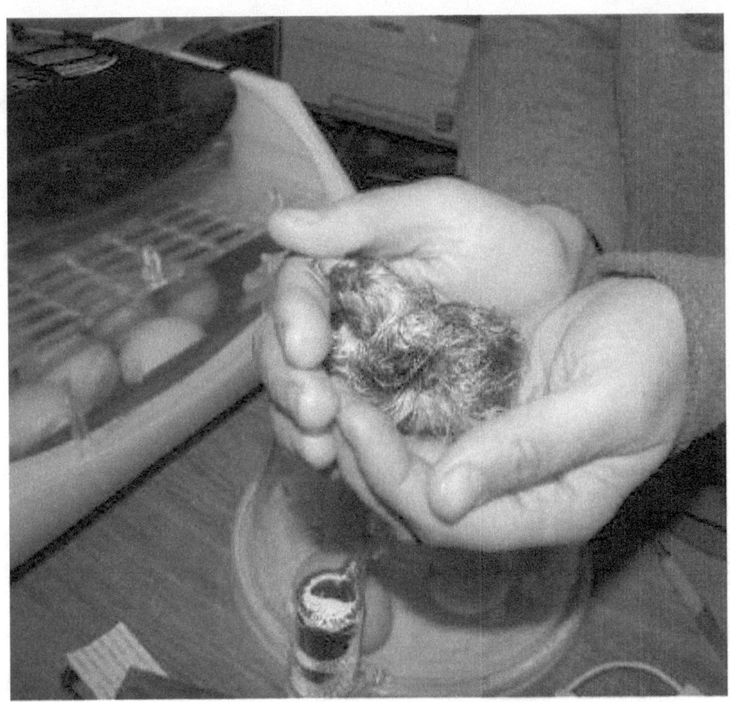

Robert Plamondon's *Success With Baby Chicks* is the only text I've come across that focuses specifically on chick care, but I was disappointed by the book's semi-commercial scale and obsession with types of brooders. Most mainstream chicken books have a section on chick care which will give you almost as much information.

Luckily, raising chicks is a lot easier than getting them out of their shells. Chicks will tell you (quite loudly) if they're unhappy. So once you learn the difference between an interested peep, a contented chuckle, an alarm trill, and a shrill "I need help" cry, you'll be an expert at chick rearing.

The more time you can spend with your chicks the better, too, since it'll be easy to notice problems if you're checking on your babies multiple times a day (and they'll get used to your presence, which helps socialize the birds). Just don't be quite as nervous of a chick mother as I was—when those newly hatched chicks topple over onto their faces, they're just taking a nap, not dying! They'll start acting more perky in a day or two.

Temperature

Temperature is the most important part of keeping your chicks healthy during their first week. If they had hatched naturally, the mother hen would have led the chicks off the nest around day two, helping them hunt for worms but also allowing the youngsters to snuggle back under her feathers every couple of minutes to keep their body temperature high. If you're raising chicks without a hen, you'll have to use some kind of artificial brooder to replace the hen's body heat.

With any kind of brooder, you should be aware that drafts can chill chicks quickly. The perfect home for a chick is well-ventilated, with air exchange at least a foot above the ground but no breeze at chick level. Especially when the chicks are young, you can achieve these conditions using an open-topped box, covered with a screen if you have young children, cats, or other predators nearby.

The most common kind of brooder is a heat lamp, which is raised or lowered to change the temperature of the chicks' home. If your room is at least 40 degrees Fahrenheit (4 degrees Celsius), you can get away with brooding up to 32 chicks under a 125-watt bulb and up to 65 chicks under a 250-watt bulb. Those chick numbers increase by 10 and 20, respectively, if the room is instead at least 60 degrees Fahrenheit (16 degrees Celsius).

However, even though they do work, heat lamps can be problematic since they use a lot of electricity, can cause fires, can blow out and allow chicks to get cold, and don't allow the chicks to maintain a natural sleep cycle. The photo on the next page shows the fire that started in our brooder when the heat lamp fell onto the bedding. To be on the safe side, secure heat lamps very carefully at least a foot above the floor of the chicks' home.

For best results, adjust the height of the lamp so that the area directly underneath is around 90 to 95 degrees Fahrenheit (32 to 35 degrees Celsius) for the first week, then decrease the temperature by 5 degrees Fahrenheit each subsequent week (which is easy to do by simply raising the lamp). You'll be able to tell if the chicks are too cold since they'll all be huddled directly under the light. Conversely, if the youngsters are too hot, they'll stay in the corners of their home. Happy chicks will be all spread out, some sleeping under the lamp while others eat, drink, and caper around.

My favorite kind of brooder is the Brinsea Ecoglow brooder, which provides a warm surface that chicks can snuggle under. (If you live in the UK, the Electric Hen seems to be a similar product.) Since this brooder heats the chick, not the room, it uses a tenth the energy of a heat lamp, and the surface never gets hot enough to start a fire. In addition, since the brooder doesn't give off light, I've found that my chicks sleep all night and seem more perky, with less troubled peeping and more studious eating and drinking during the day. Choose between the small brooder (good for 20 chicks) and the large brooder (for up to 50 chicks). And raise the brooder up every week to allow larger chicks underneath.

No matter what you use to keep your chicks warm, be sure to keep the heat source in place for at least three weeks; slower-growing chicks in cold weather might need a brooder for up to six weeks. My rule of thumb is that once chicks have replaced all of their fuzz with real feathers, they're ready to heat themselves as long as the temperature in their coop doesn't drop below freezing.

Finally, be prepared for power outages. Especially during their first week of life, half an hour without an external supply of heat can be enough to kill your tender chicks. A chemical hand warmer or a hot-water bottle might be enough to tide the chicks over until the juice comes back on if the air temperature isn't too chilly.

Food and water

Chicks don't need to eat or drink during their first three days of life, which is how they can be shipped through the mail with few losses. Once mail-order chicks arrive on your doorstep, though, they need to start eating and drinking immediately. So many owners take the time to dip chick beaks one by one in the water dish and to show chicks individually to their feeder.

Homegrown chicks are much easier in this regard. I have food and water ready in their brooder as soon as they hatch, and my chicks learn to eat and drink by themselves. They usually spend 12 to 24 hours sleeping off their exertions after a hatch, after which point the strongest chicks quickly discover the food and water. All of the other chicks soon follow suit.

If your chicks come before you've made it to the store, they can subsist quite happily on hard-boiled eggs (cut into bite-size pieces) for a few days. However, you'll probably want to buy starter feed (a mixture of grains, soybeans, and minerals) from your feed store.

Assuming you're willing to put in a bit of effort to keep your chicks from eating their own feces (see the housing section and the information about nipple waterers below), you won't need medicated feed. But you might have to specifically ask for non-medicated feed. Giving your chicks med-icated feed won't hurt them, but you do risk eating the residual chemicals in their eggs and meat and might find it in the compost from their bedding.

Chicks should be allowed to eat as much as they want for at least the first few weeks, but they'll waste a lot of feed by scratching it out of the dish if you feed them in an open container. I've had good luck filling a one-cup plastic container with feed and cut-ting head-sized holes in the lid to give the chicks plenty of access to food without allowing them to spill any.

After a week or so, I move the chicks to a larger coop that houses the store-bought automatic feeder shown on the next page. Be sure to allow a trough length large enough so sthat chicks won't fight over their feed.

The table below gives recommended feed amounts per chick over the course of their childhood. These figures are based on heirloom laying breeds—Cornish Cross grow much faster and eat a lot more.

Chick age (weeks)	Pounds per chick per week
0-1	0.1
1.1 - 2	0.2
2.1 - 3	0.3
3.1 - 4	0.4
4.1 - 5	0.5
5.1 - 6	0.6
6.1 - 7	0.7
7.1 - 8	0.8
8.1 - 9	0.9
9.1 - 10	1.0
10.1 - 11	1.1
11.1 - 12	1.1
12.1 - 13	1.2
13.1 - 14	1.2
14.1 - 15	1.2
15.1 - 16	1.3

You might choose to keep track of how much feed your chickens are consuming to help you determine whether they're wasting food, whether pasture is cutting your feed costs, and the chicks' feed-to-meat ratio (for broilers).

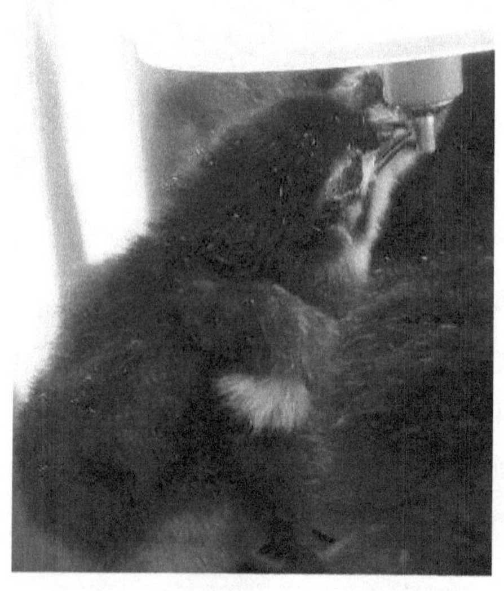

Clean water is also essential for chicks since fouled water can spread disease. In addition, you need to ensure that chicks don't drown in open waterers during their first week of life and that water doesn't dampen the bedding, which leads to the spread of coccidiosis and other diseases. My husband and I strongly believe that nipple waterers make chicks happier and healthier. But you can get away with something much simpler as long as you clean the water frequently, raise its height regularly, and put marbles in open waterers for the first week to prevent drowning.

Housing

Everyone houses their chicks a bit differently. I like to keep ours in a very small container in the living room for their first week, then I move them to a larger outdoor chick coop. The first photo on the next page shows the Rubbermaid container we use to house our chicks for their first few days, while the other photos in this section illustrate our outdoor coop.

Some important questions to consider when planning chick housing include:

Will your chicks be warm and dry? Especially for their first three weeks of life, chicks can't handle even a little bit of rain splashing into their living area. The best outdoor chick coops are raised slightly off the ground so that flooding during heavy rains can't get the inside wet. In addition, you may want to insulate some or all of the coop if you're raising chicks outdoors in cold weather. At the other extreme, you might need to install extra vents or fans if you're raising chicks during hot weather.

Can you make the coop very small for the first few days so the chicks don't stumble away from the heat and get lost? Cardboard dividers work well to enclose chicks within a larger space, allowing you to expand their living area a bit at a time over a week or two. After that, more space is better than less, with chicks requiring at least 0.5 square feet apiece for their first month of life, then 1, 2, and 3 square feet apiece for their second, third, and fourth months. If your chicks can go outside, they'll require less room inside.

Will your chicks have access to sunlight? Young chicks love to lounge in the sun, and artificial lighting isn't the same. Make sure your coop has at least one window that allows sunlight to stream in for part or all of the day. However, make sure  the sunny window doesn't cause the coop to overheat.

Is your chick coop somewhere you can check on it often? Chicks who are right outside your front door will fare better than those down at the barn (plus they'll be better socialized). My husband built a plexiglass wall onto one side of our outdoor brooder so we could watch the chicks from our kitchen window even after they moved outside.

Do you want to allow chicks on pasture at an early age? Many people keep their chicks inside for a month or two before letting them out on pasture, but I believe chicks are healthier (and become better foragers) if they have access to greenery as early as possible. Chicks don't take well to being transported outside every day and then back in for the night. So if you want them to be on pasture at a young age, you'll want to build an outdoor chick coop.

Is your coop completely predator-proof? Make sure that there are no holes more than an inch in diameter in your chick coop. (That may mean you need to screen ventilation holes or windows.) Otherwise, rats will be attracted to the free-choice feed and will find your chicks too tasty to pass up. Snakes are another common predator of young chicks, as are household cats and dogs. Our losses to predators plummeted to zero even in outdoor coops after I started shutting the chicks in each evening and opening their door back up in the morning.

How will you keep the coop from smelling? I recommend deep litter since it has been shown to keep chickens healthier than any other manure-management system. Deep litter consists of filling the bottom of your coop with three to six inches of straw, dried wood shavings, or (my favorite option) tree leaves. Whenever you start to notice manure on the surface of the bedding or catch any hint of a foul odor, add a bit more bedding on top. No matter what you do, don't bed young chicks on a slick surface or they'll develop spraddle legs.

Do chicks need perches? Not really, but most lighter-weight breeds will enjoy having something to hop up onto by the time they're two or three weeks old. We use sticks out of the woods, and place the first practice perches just a couple of inches off the ground, with more higher up. Don't worry if your chicks refuse to use the perches, though—some breeds are simply more flighty than others.

Pasturing chicks

A later volume in the Permaculture Chicken series covers pasturing adult chickens in great depth. But many folks think chicks don't need pasture until they're a month old and ready to leave the brooder, so I wanted to include a brief note in this book to tell you that chicks thrive when bugs and leafy greens supplement their store-bought diet. There's no need to worry you'll overdo it—chicks will naturally eat just as much wild food as they need and no more.

The biggest concern with pasturing very young chicks is that you'll lose some to predators or that the chicks will get lost or wet. I keep young chicks right outside my door and don't let them onto pasture until they're big enough that they won't slip through my temporary fence material. I'm also careful to keep their pasture very small (no bigger than the coop) for at least a few days, expanding their foraging ground a bit at a time in the same way I did with their inside area during their first two weeks of life. Finally, I spend an hour or two with the chicks each time I expand their pasture to make sure no one gets lost or upset. We have a ramp to allow chicks easy access to the coop, and we graze them in an area with some bushes and tall plants to hide among in case a hawk makes an appearance.

Before they're ready to go out on pasture, I hand-gather tidbits for my miniature flock. Very young chicks (two weeks old or less) like weed flowers best of all—blooms of purple dead nettle, tick-trefoil, and sourgrass are all consumed quickly. They'll also eat some leaves, although their lack of teeth makes it easier for chicks to swallow leafy foods when the plants are attached to the ground

and can be pecked apart. Tender and small leaves are chick favorites—sourgrass again (especially in the summer when other plants are tougher), young bluegrass leaves, and (especially on pasture) white clover. In the summer, I also gather young tick-trefoil seed heads since my chicks will eat the seeds after scarfing down the flowers.

Invertebrates are very nutritious, but are hard for a chick to eat by itself. A mother hen pecks worms and bugs apart to make it easier for chicks to scarf them down, but my vigorous chicks can eat skinny earthworms by fighting over the wrigglers until the worms are broken into bite-size pieces.

Young chicks aren't able to scratch up heavy mulch, so they can coexist with most vegetable gardens until they're one to two months old (depending on the chicken breed). If you want to make them happy, turn over logs to give chicks access to extra invertebrates. Or graze them under the fruit trees in your yard for pest control.

Growing up

As your chicks mature, they'll need more food and water and lots more room. If you're utilizing deep bedding, you should top off the bedding material more often to keep the coop from smelling, and nipple waterers will need to be raised a notch every week or so to keep them at beak level.

Once your chicks are old enough that they don't need supplemental heat, you may want to move them to a full-size chicken coop. If you're mixing chicks in with adult chickens, consider building a creep feeder so the chicks don't get bullied away from the feed by their elders, and keep an eye on the combined flock for a few days to make sure the chicks don't get picked on.

Most people eat broilers at 8 weeks (for fast-growing Cornish Cross) or between 12 and 16 weeks (for slower-growing breeds). If the chickens are keepers, both pullets (girls) and cockerels (boys) become sexually mature when they are between 4 and 6 months old. That means your pullets will start laying eggs (as long as they don't reach maturity in the winter) and your cockerels can fertilize eggs. Now you're ready for another round of incubating homegrown eggs!

Index

About the author

I hope this book saves you lots of trial and error and that you end up with happy, healthy chicks. After you give the contents a try, you'll make my day if you take a minute to leave a review on the retailer of your choice.

Then, if you want to delve deeper into the world of efficient and environmentally friendly chicken keeping, there are several other volumes available in my Permaculture Chicken series. Raw beginners should start with the FREE *Getting Started With Your Working Chicken*. Then you can learn to optimize your flocks' pasture, build a poop-free chicken waterer, feed yourself from your flock, and dive deeper into variety selection in the rest of the series. Head over to https://wetknee.com/chickens/ for more information.

Finally, I hope you'll join my email list at https://wetknee.com/free-books/ for monthly homesteading tips, information about new releases, and a free ebook.

Thank you for reading. You are why I write.